Chinese Home Cooking

The Easy Cookbook to Prepare Over 100 Tasty, Traditional Wok and Modern Chinese Recipes at Home

By

Adele Tyler

© **Copyright 2020 by Adele Tyler- All rights reserved.**

This document is geared towards providing exact and reliable information in regards to the topic and issue covered. The publication is sold with the idea that the publisher is not required to render accounting, officially permitted, or otherwise, qualified services. If advice is necessary, legal or professional, a practiced individual in the profession should be ordered.

- From a Declaration of Principles which was accepted and approved equally by a Committee of the American Bar Association and a Committee of Publishers and Associations.

It is not legal in any way to reproduce, duplicate, or transmit any part of this document in either electronic means or in printed format. Recording of this publication is strictly prohibited and any storage of this document is not allowed unless with written permission from the publisher. All rights reserved.

The information provided herein is stated to be truthful and consistent, in that any liability, in terms of inattention or otherwise, by any usage or abuse of any policies, processes, or directions contained within is the solitary and utter responsibility of the recipient reader. Under no circumstances will any legal responsibility or blame be held against the publisher for any reparation, damages, or monetary loss due to the information herein, either directly or indirectly.

Respective authors own all copyrights not held by the publisher.

The information herein is offered for informational purposes solely, and is universal as so. The presentation of the information is without contract or any type of guarantee assurance.

The trademarks that are used are without any consent, and the publication of the trademark is without permission or backing by the trademark owner. All trademarks and brands within this book are for clarifying purposes only and are owned by the owners themselves, not affiliated with this document.

Table of Contents

INTRODUCTION 7

CHAPTER 1: ORIGIN AND HISTORICAL BACKGROUND OF CHINESE FOOD 10

1.1 History of Traditional Chinese Dishes 13

1.2 Evolution of Chinese Cuisine 17

1.3 Rise of Chinese Food's Popularity in the United States 21

CHAPTER 2: COOKING METHODS AND HEALTH BENEFITS OF CHINESE FOOD 24

2.1 Preparing Chinese Food at Home vs. Eating at Restaurants 24

2.2 Health Benefits of Chinese Food 27

2.3 Specific Cooking Techniques Used in Chinese Restaurants 29

CHAPTER 3: CHINESE APPETIZERS AND BREAKFAST RECIPES 32

3.1 Delicious Chinese Appetizer Recipes 32

3.2 Chinese Breakfast Recipes 44

CHAPTER 4: CHINESE LUNCH AND SNACK RECIPES .. 58

4.1 Chinese Snack Recipes 58

4.2 Chinese Lunch Recipes 68

CHAPTER 5: CHINESE DINNER AND DESSERT RECIPES 86

5.1 Dinner Recipes of Chinese Cuisine 86

5.2 Chinese Desserts Recipes..99

CHAPTER 6: CHINESE TRADITIONAL WOK RECIPES AND VEGETARIAN CHINESE MEALS 112

6.1 Chinese Famous Wok Recipes 112

6.2 World Renowned Chinese Recipes 124

6.3 Recipes of Vegetarian Chinese Meals..138

CONCLUSION 151

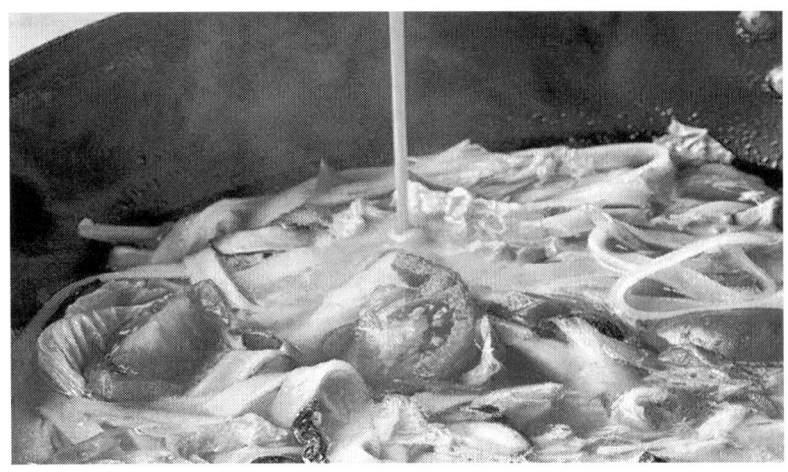

Introduction

Chinese cuisine developed from different areas of China and soon became very popular around the world for its unique cooking style and flavor. There are eight central cuisines in china. Chinese foods are mainly comprised of two components that are grains and meat. Starch and vegetables are essential ingredients of all dishes. The necessary foundation of the most Chinese dishes is garlic, ginger, and sesame. Soy sauce is used in all cuisines for saltiness.

Stir-frying is an essential technique to cook Chinese cuisines. A wok is used to stir-fry vegetables in garlic. Wok dishes are the most common and widespread in America. Chinese cuisine got popular when Chinese immigrants came to America and worked in food shops.

Many traditional Chinese dishes gained popularity in America. Thus, many chefs in the United States made a bit changes in Chinese cooking style, hence Chinese-American dishes emerged.

Chinese cuisine is not only tasty but also healthy and nutritious. Spices used in Chinese cooking are full of nutrients that a human body needs to work the whole day. These are a rich source of carbohydrates, starch, proteins, and fibers. This book "Chinese Home Cooking" will explain Chinese cuisine and its early history. The first chapter will introduce Chinese food and its emergence from the Zhou dynasty to the Ming Dynasty, how it has evolved from time to time, and has become famous in the United States.

The second chapter is a brief discussion about the benefits of the Chinese cuisine. Moreover, it will help you enhance your cooking skills through specific techniques used in Chinese restaurants. This chapter will also tell you the difference between Chinese traditional home cooking and restaurant cooking style. The third chapter is about breakfast and appetizer recipes to make you start your day with delicious and quick recipes. The fourth Chapter is about lunch and snack recipes to regain the energy you have wasted during your work. The fifth chapter includes dinner and dessert recipes to make tasty food for your family meal with some sweet dishes and side dishes.

The last chapter will provide you three different kinds of meals, including traditional wok recipes, famous recipes known worldwide, and, the most importantly, vegetarian recipes. You can choose to make these recipes in your special events or family gatherings.

Finally, a brief conclusion about choosing Chinese cuisine for you and your family are given to help you support your idea of selecting Chinese food.

So, start reading this book and enhance your cooking knowledge and cooking skills with "Chinese Home Cooking".

Chapter 1: Origin and Historical Background of Chinese Food

China is the country with the most prominent citizens and the nation with the highest and most innovative cuisine in the world. The general name for dishes from different regions and ethnicities in China is Chinese cuisine. With excellent infrastructure, rich divisions and institutions, and a distinctive theme, it has a long history. It is the crystallization of the past of thousands of years of Chinese cuisine. A significant aspect of Chinese culture, also known as the Chinese culinary tradition, is Chinese cuisine. Chinese cuisine is one of the triple international cuisines and has a far-reaching influence on the East Asian region. The ingredients are sourced from different areas and cultural dishes.

Chinese Cuisine in the Zhou Dynasty

According to ancient records, China already had a barbecue, fried fish, and other foods more than 5000 years ago.

Food was primarily grains such as peas, buckwheat, corn, and brown rice during the Zhou dynasty in China, although they were not the same as what we have produced in the modern agricultural industry today. In the late Zhou dynasty, people began to get white rice/peeling rice, which was very rare and expensive and affordable for the wealthy class to consume. Similar to other countries, salt was a key factor in cooking and people's everyday life. By then, salt was widely used already. There was a popular cuisine called 'Ba Zheng' in the Zhou Dynasty, which was quite popular for centuries to come.

Chinese Cuisine in the Qin Dynasty

In the Qin dynasty, the sour taste was accepted by the people at a certain time. Bamboo slides recovered from temples, according to historical documents, berries were another hot cooking by then. It was primarily used for extracting fishy unusual from meat or fish inferred by academics. Besides, during the Qin dynasty, cinnamon, spring onions, canola source, and cider were also used in the cooking.

Chinese Cuisine in Han Dynasty

When it came to the Han dynasty, salty taste was preferred. Han was a time when Chinese cuisine took a major move forward. There were many "foreign-made" food and cooking ingredients for people at the period, such as peppers, grapefruit, oranges, hazelnuts, cardamom, pineapple, pomegranate, broccoli, lettuce, thyme, fennel, spinach, garlic, and onion, owing to the opening of the Silk Road in the Han Dynasty, for traders and commercial trade. In the later tang dynasty, this lay a strong cornerstone for the advances of Chinese cuisine. Chinese cuisine quickly evolved during the Han, Wei, northern and Southern Dynasties, and many popular cuisines emerged.

Chinese Cuisine in Tang Dynasty

Chinese cuisine had already grown to a standard of quality by the period of the Tang dynasty. People also had several types of gatherings or cocktail parties to live their time at a certain period.

Chinese Cuisine in the Song Dynasty

The Song Dynasty is among the stars of the history of Chinese cuisine. There were various cold meals, hot meals, soups, and decorative dishes at Bianjing and Linen's menus. The dishes were labeled with North, South, Chuan flavors, and vegetable meals, which indicated that cuisines' institutions started to develop.

Chinese Cuisine in Yuan, Ming, and Qing Dynasty

During the Yuan, Ming, and Qing Dynasty, Chinese cuisine had a huge success. Hundreds of cuisines emerged. During this time, ethnicities believed in Islamism, migrated to all parts of China, and halal certification occupied China's role as a new form of Chinese food. Since the Qing Dynasty was a king ruling under the Manchu people, Manchu style and flavors were introduced to Chinese cuisine. During the Ming Dynasty of this time frame, chilled pepper crops were introduced as an elegant plant in China. It did not take too long until Chinese people learned its high benefit in cooking methods. The spicy flavor soon became popular in Hunan and Sichuan provinces at that period and had since left a massive impact on their cooking style. Chinese cuisine schools were founded. From the late Qing Dynasty and outsiders came to China, Chinese cuisine even added some characteristics of western cuisines. In the world, Chinese cuisine is very popular for its color, scent, flavor, and better style.

1.1 History of Traditional Chinese Dishes

Chinese cooking is commonly seen to represent one of the country's wealthiest and most varied cuisine histories and cultures. It emerged in various areas of China, and it has been spread from Southeast Asia to Western Europe and North America to other regions of the world. In Chinese culture, dinner is usually seen as made up of two specific components: (1) a source of starch or carbohydrate and (2) fruit, seafood, pork, or other things corresponding meals.

Rice is a vital component of much of Chinese food, as it is widely known globally. Wheat-based items like noodles and boiled buns play a large role in comparison to South China, where rice is prevalent. Despite the value of rice in Chinese cuisine, it is always the case that no grain would be provided at all on highly formal events; in such a scenario; rice will be offered only if all other dishes existed, or as a consolation dish at the end of dinner. To relieve one's stomach, soup is usually eaten at the end of dinner. Serving soup at the beginning of a meal is still very common nowadays, owing to Western influences.

Chinese cuisine history dates back to approximately 5000 BC. Chinese people have created their special way of cooking meat over this large period. Their ways of defining ingredients to make ideal combos, their multi-method cooking strategies, and their multidisciplinary flavoring management have all been increasingly improved. There was a very good diet for the ancient Chinese, and from historical records, agriculture in China appears to have begun around 5,000 years ago. Both variations and transitions are marked by Chinese cuisine. Since ancient times, food has been at the heart of social life, and many current-day dishes with their variations of fragrance and flavor can be linked back to ancient Chinese food patterns.

Food and art have often been regarded by the Chinese, emphasizing preparing food and how it is consumed.

Chopsticks are the main dining utensil for real food in Chinese culture, while sauces and other fluids are enjoyed with a large, flat-bottomed (historically stainless) spoon. Due to the recent deforestation deficits in china and other Asian countries, wooden chopsticks are decreasing their supremacy; many Chinese dining facilities are considering switching to a more environmentally friendly eating fork and spoon, such as plastics or bamboo chopsticks. In the past, more luxurious items used included silver and gold. On the other side, in small restaurants, plastic chopsticks crafted of bamboo/wood have all replaced recycled ones.

Vegetables: Soy Bean and Cucumber

There were not many types of veggies in ancient China, but vegetables were an important part of people's diets regardless. They consumed vegetables with their main meal, rice, whenever they were able to afford it. During that time, the main vegetables were cucumber and soybean, and when soybeans had become the main grain in ancient China, soybean production can be dated back to 1000 BC. The word Shu means soybean began appearing on brass artifacts from the early Zhou period. Soybeans were also described in the Analects of Confucius in the 5th century BC.

Wine: Rice and Millet

China is considered to be one of the earliest countries to produce wine in the world. Wine has not only been a beverage since its launch, but has also been provided with moral and cultural importance, representing political and social life and design concepts, and even appearing in modern literature.

People started to drink wine during the Shang dynasty (16th to 12th century) and used it to honor the deities; yellow grain wine is probably the first of this kind.

Since the Han and Tang dynasties, all other types of wine are believed to have been produced. Millet wine was released years later, and it was a major success, much more common than tea.

Sorghum

The "camel of crops" is classified as sorghum since it does not require much moisture and develops in the soil in which other grains do not. Also, the cost of grain and fertilizer for sorghum is smaller than for other crops. Dating back to the Stone Age is the use of sorghum. A significant volume of carbonized sorghum was detected from the feuding State Period in Shijiazhuang. "China is the oldest and greatest Centre for the roots of sorghum," according to the Genomic Resources Center.

Meat: Pork, Chicken, Beef

Pork is China's most widely-eaten meat, including beef, mutton, goat, duck, bird, etc., and other kinds. From 3000 or 4000 BC, the people in china consumed pork, which was indigenous to China, but cattle and sheep were not indigenous, and soon after that they were imported in China from West Asia. Many people used tofu, or bean paste, as a dietary protein source because the beef was too pricey and because Buddhist monks did not consume meat.

Tea

The origin of Chinese tea can be measured to 4,000 years. The Chinese probably drink tea to be an elegant form of art with so many traditions and traditions attached to it. Tea, along with espresso and cocoa, is China's national beverage and is one of the three popular sweet drinks. China firmly considers itself the cradle of tea as China was the first nation to bring its planting strategies, manufacturing, and drinking practices to the rest of the globe.

Tofu

Tofu, or bean paste, is also of Chinese ancestry and is made from soy protein, milk, water, and a coagulating agent. It has been a dietary staple in Chinese and Asian food since prehistoric times, abundant in minerals, low in fat, and full of protein, calcium, and iron. Since it was a great source of vitamins, Chinese doctors considered that meat was an important meal, but only the wealthiest could afford to consume it. A bill was made to remedy this, where any person living in China will get a free cup of tofu each week, which was a combination of sorghum and other stuff like rice to give everyone the same amount of protein as the meat will. It was hard to cook on a massive scale in China at that time, so people might cut their meat into tiny pieces to prepare it. In Western vegetable meals even, tofu has also become a primary ingredient.

Wheat

People began developing and consuming wheat in China about 2500 BC, previously dependent on exports from West Asia, wheat soon became the primary source of carbohydrates. The traditional Chinese people consumed porridge, but they made no bread out of wheat. The key factor for this was that to cook the rolls, the coal they used for the energy was too pricey.

Rice

Rice is indeed a good source of carbohydrates, comparable to millet, grain, and other crops. In China, rice background goes back to the late Stone Age (around 2000 BC). Rice production is believed to have begun in Thailand, but Chinese farmers invented grain rice.

The method of rice cultivation in muddy, natural ponds is called rice paddies.

Rice was used as a commodity in China since prehistoric times, and when we think of Chinese cuisine, rice is most certainly the very first thing you say of. While rice has been growing in China for a long time, that was too cool to grow rice in north china, so wheat and soybeans were farmed anyway. People cooked rice to render it softer by boiling or steaming it, and rice was also used to create a sort of wine called rice wine, which is still drunk in China today.

1.2 Evolution of Chinese Cuisine

The history of Chinese food covers three centuries of recorded history, spanning an unprecedented expansion of food preparations, food preparation methods, and the use of tons of ingredients.

History of Chinese Noodles

One of the important steps of their whole cuisine is Chinese boiling noodles. They can be located within countless recipes in hundreds of combinations, which has sparked the improvements in cooking style over the Chinese country's history and national tastes. The earliest recorded noodles discovered in China date back 4,000 years. They have been found in historical discoveries along China's Yellow River. However, the first definite historical records of noodles are from the period around 25 to 200 AD. when the East Han Dynasty ruled. These early noodles were traditionally made from corn flour, and as years went by, they became even more common. In the Song Dynasty period, noodles could be bought from Chinese restaurants in major cities in China. Noodles are extensively used in China, Korea, the Philippines, Cambodia, Thailand, Vietnam, and others as Chinese presence spread throughout Asia.

One of the three major components is typical noodles made in China: white flour, corn starch, and mung bean flour. They are sliced using one of the five methods until they are baked and used as a component of other foods: Sliced (with the blade from rolled bread sheet), compressed (dough moved by the device into tiny holes), Peel (large bread strips are cut straight into hot water), Pulled (squeezed dough folded to produce thinner layers) and mashed (rolled bread to the shape desired). Without any hesitation, Char kway teow, Cup Noodles Ban mien, Cart noodle, Beef chow fun, Laksa, Lo mien, Zhejiang mien, and Re gan mien are the most common dishes in Chinese food that use noodles.

History of Chinese Sweet Food

Chinese cuisine has become one of the best diverse globally with an amazing array of dairy products invented by Chinese chefs and developed by more than Three thousand years of things change, proximity to trade channels, and local food products availability. China has managed to produce a wide range of desserts, in contrast to thousands of recognizable dishes and a wide range of liquid drinks (both distilled and unsweetened), which can be made on both prepared foods such as fruit and more complex recipes, often requiring preparation that can last many months or years.

Chinese sweets are delicious, but typically with less amount of sugar than Western deserts. They also have a greater proportion of natural fruit products, which can be used as an integral part of the Chinese Ying and Yang custom of consuming "healthy" meals, not only during dinners and with coffee, but also during meal options.

Chinese desserts are typically classified into several major groups, such as pastry products, candy products (including baked wheat goods such as Moon pastries), candies, cookies, rice-based treats, sweet flavorings, desert meringues, caramels, and ice creams.

Traditional Chinese sweets also played a significant role in upholding Chinese lifestyles and the nutrition of many Asian countries, which have established a cultural and economic relationship with China, making Chinese desserts much more popular and broader.

History of Chinese Soups

China has a long tradition of using many kinds of soups in its kitchen, almost always cooked and eaten to provide the meal with nutrition and provide nutrition and be a provider of natural and therapeutic herbs that can improve the vitality and immune function. Although western soups can contain daily products (dairy products or cream) from start to end, Chinese soups are often broth-based, thickened by refined starches of maize or sweet potatoes.

Chinese Pickles History

A big part of the local food is Chinese pickles. In certain variants, fermented veggies or berries are available because Chinese people usually do not consume fresh fruits. They tend to eat them fried, baked, and processed in several other ways, and if food is poorly handled, the processing is better for many reasons, most important. In China, pickled food is processed by soaking and roasting in salt or brine vegetables and fruits instead of fermenting in paste or sauce compounds. Along with a wide range of medicinal herbs and several other components (even beers), it is very popular to dissolve fruits and vegetables in the pickling method. It should be remembered that mainstream medicine and research do not suggest that many marinated foods be used in their everyday diets. Some researchers have found that marinated food can increase cancer risks, and even marinated vegetables have been reported as possible carcinogens by the World Health Organization. Pickled food could also get riddled with different fungi species very quickly, which can increase the carcinogenic potential of certain foods much further.

Chinese Tea History

Tea holds the most significant position in the Chinese cuisine development, having been present in its society for more than 3,000 years and gradually evolving to its present form with each moving century. Chinese heritage holds the evidence of the first tea drinking during the Zhou Dynasty, stretching back to the third century BC, with various reports confirming that they have been used mainly as medicines since the earliest days. The rich noble's use of tea as a treat and community drink helped popularize in the 8th and 9th centuries during the Tang Dynasty. The style of tea preparing, serving, rituals, protocol, procedures, and even cookware used has altered many Chinese imperial dynasties. The Song Dynasty (960-1276, tea pancakes that were ground into flour and combined with warm water) and the Ming Dynasty (1368-1644, Hiqiu tea, song Luo tea, and several others) were the two most important royal dynasties that made popular the dissemination of new varieties of tea throughout Asia. In the late 1700s, new forms of Chinese tea began to grow under the Qing Dynasty.

Chinese tea varieties can be distinguished between trees, regions that have been grown, and processed. Today, beyond any doubt, the most common form of tea is Chinese Green Tea, produced from the "Camellia Sinensis" herb and manufactured with limited oxidation. Not just because of its good taste and body feel, but because of its medicinal qualities that can minimize the risk of cardiovascular disease and certain forms of cancer, improve the metabolism, and this tea was more praised in China.

1.3 Rise of Chinese Food's Popularity in the United States

The first big influx of Asian refugees to America was the "Chinese 49'ers" who settled in the United States a century before the American Revolutionary War and grafted the first Asian food to America. The first multicultural cuisine at the national scale to be heavily commercialized as a form of food specifically cooked and eaten away from family was Chinese food. Food from China started to draw a fast-growing non-Asian customer base of varied different ethnicities in major cities throughout the nation at the turn of the nineteenth century, and Chinese food became the most popular multicultural cuisine throughout the United States by 1980, helped by the resurgence of Chinese immigration to the United States. As one of the two primary sources of jobs for Chinese immigrants and communities for centuries, Chinese cuisine has also been a critical economic lifesaver for Chinese Americans. Hence, its creation is a significant chapter in United States history and a core part of Chinese America's understanding. The numerous and sometimes disparate developments in the United States the Chinese food industry shows that it is currently at an intersection. The future depends on the degree to which Chinese Americans will dramatically shift their impact on the social and political arena and on the willingness of China in its relationship between the two countries to alter the financial system.

The Transplantation of Chinese Food

When the 49'ers entered California through China, Chinese food landed in America in the major gold period, illustrating immigrants' crucial role in implanting regional food to America.

Not because they wished to evangelize their cuisine amongst non-Chinese, but because of its exceptional significance in establishing their culture and identity, Chinese immigrants took their cuisine to the New World.

The implantation of Chinese food coincided with the development of Chinese societies. During this time, food companies represented a critical sector in the ethnic Chinese industry in major California cities, such as San Diego and San Fran. Thirty-three supermarkets, along with seven hotels and five food stores, accounted for almost half of all firms in the developing Chinese settlement of San Francisco in 1857, outstripping all other forms of enterprises. While in the 1870s, laundry stores in San Diego and San Francisco soon outnumbered Chinese food companies, the former were dispersed in numerous parts of their respective localities. By contrast, within Chinatown, the latter was the central component of exchange and established its significance.

Chinese restaurants selling foods became another significant draw for Chinese immigrants in Chinatown and exposed the fundamental importance of food to the Chinese culture. Indeed, the arrival of Chinese restaurants has often marked the start of a society. For instance, in 1849, in San Francisco, four restaurants launched an emerging culture. In the developing Chinese communities in other towns, such as Marysville, restaurants were also present. It was a major Chinese village site, also known as the larger town (san bu) among the Chinese. There were already three restaurants and two Chinese shops in 1853. At inexpensive rates, Chinese restaurants deliver historically recognized cuisine. In the late 1870s, migrants like Ah Quin could buy a meal for as little as 10 cents in San Fran's Chinatown. However, Chinese dining establishments provided a culturally significant room to relax and socialize. The Chicago Post described a respectable Chinese restaurant in the center as "the resort and gathering room of East Asiatic".

The Birth of "Chinese-American Cuisine"

At the beginning of the 20th century, as Chinese restaurants penetrated to non-Chinese neighborhoods, the third stage in Chinese food development and its popularity in America started to establish an omnipotent presence across the country. As a paper published in 1903, "there is scarcely an American city that did not have its Chinese restaurants to which people of all classes want to go." The proliferation of Chinese restaurants beyond Chinatown during this time created a special Chinese cuisine for American customers. The distribution of Chinese food gained from two important interactions that many Chinese Americans had in the service industry: first, their role as household work, which gave them great knowledge of serving food to a non-Chinese customer base; second, their role as laundrymen, from which they knew how to enabled service in non-Chinese neighborhoods.

Not middle-class visitors and affluent enthusiasts, but white people on the fringes of society, such as hippies, African Americans, and refugees like Jews from Eastern Europe, were the customers who helped make Chinese food into the first non-Anglo cuisine to gain national popularity in popular consumption. Unlike the middle-class visitors who, out of interest, dined in Chinatown cafes, these more oppressed Americans became the most loyal customer base, regularly visiting these restaurants inside and outside Chinatown. The latter two parties sponsored Chinese dining institutions in various East Coast cities. "The New York Tribune reported in 1901, describing the importance of Chinese food amongst the less fortunate, "So many who, though having a limited share of the products of this country, still impact 'sportiness' visit the restaurant for its cheapness and rise to enjoy the strongly flavorful dishes. Chinese food gained little intellectual recognition until recently, because of its historical importance and pervasive appearance.

Chapter 2: Cooking Methods and Health Benefits of Chinese Food

Chinese food usually includes those vegetables and spices that are very nutritious and good for health. Although many different and unique techniques to prepare Chinese cuisine at home and restaurants are there. The ingredients used in the Chinese food are rich in carbohydrates, fiber, proteins, and calcium. This chapter will provide you information about different restaurants' techniques to prepare food and the health benefits of the ingredients they use.

2.1 Preparing Chinese Food at Home vs. Eating at Restaurants

The food that is served at home is very close to that served in China's restaurants.

Restaurant food appears to be cooked more intricately than one would usually do at home.

Restaurants often tend to be more creative when making variants on a cooking method, whereas organic cuisine is more conventional and sticks to the standard recipe rigidly. This is only a consequence, though, of one person being a professionally skilled cook, and the other being a distracted wife/husband. China is a large country, and the cuisine has a great deal of variation from region to region.

In comparison, Chinese meals served in restaurants appear to be less nutritious than real Chinese foods available at home. Chefs can do less for the ingredients that their consumers eat, whether it be high sugar or unhealthy fat, which can be seen at any restaurant. Many restaurants buy inexpensive goods to make a full profit while Chinese foods eaten at home are made from the finest and freshest products. Restaurants will usually use an assortment of liquids and herbs to make these dishes taste healthier. While these restaurant dishes may be extremely tasty, they are not as flavorful and delicious as home-cooked meals because they are normally miss-sauced, too much-salted, or sometimes over-rich.

The Chinese food we see in local New York restaurants is somewhat different from the typical Chinese food in Chinese households. The products used are the key contrast between conventional and American Chinese foods. Many American Chinese restaurants replace conventional ingredients for those available in the surrounding areas to cater to the community's citizens. American Chinese diets focus on meats instead of including vegetables such as rice, pasta, and sorghum, including steamed veggies as side dishes.

Thus, restaurants have a huge amount of content to pick from when writing their meals.

On the table, there are sometimes dishes that people don't know how to prepare or have never consumed before only because they are the dishes that are lifted from another part of China.

As many western restaurants modify Chinese and Indian cuisine to fit a western pallet, Chinese restaurants adjust dishes from other regions to meet the local preferences. Thus, if in a style bar, the food you see in the restaurant may be nothing like the typical home-cooked recipe as the chef must have modified it.

One meal that is used in nearly every restaurant is pork over grain. Much as Americans want it, the dish's main emphasis is the pork, using rice to bring variation to the meal. While American Chinese products include corn, they sometimes replace more Western vegetables such as carrot, broccoli, cabbage, tomatoes, and dairy products for the other main vegetables used. The process used in cooking and serving the food is another extremely significant contrast between Chinese domestic cooking and cafeteria cooking. Considering the vast quantities of food that restaurants have to prepare during a normal working day, many restaurants start cooking food the day before delivering it.

Much as restaurant-style and Chinese house style cooking cuisine vary in the products used and in the preparing processes, they also vary in the cooking types overall. Chinese cuisine foods, ranging from simmering to frying, can be cooked in any manner that the person likes. However, most dishes are cooked by frying techniques in Chinese restaurants, using either a wok, a round-bottomed frying container used for stir-frying, or a cooking pot. Even traditional Chinese foods discovered at home commonly use other ways, such as simmering, to cook rice. Usually, Chinese domestic style cooking is much healthy but lacks the taste that can be seen in cooking in the restaurant-style.

2.2 Health Benefits of Chinese Food

Chinese food is very famous, and it contains all the nutrition that a sound metabolism and body require to remain healthy. While Chinese people consume, on average, thirty percent more calories than Americans, and they have the same behavior patterns, they do not have obesity issues. This is because fructose and vitamin free food are avoided in Chinese cuisine.

Vegetables are "add-ons" to other recipes in the West, but vegetables are key in Chinese cuisine. Chinese assume the significant proportion of vegetables can be properly combined with a minor portion of livestock. Meat is important since excess calories are incorporated. Sugar, processed sugars, and high fat ingredients are quite less in Chinese foods, allowing our bodies to know quickly when they are full. This encourages people who consume Chinese food to survive more on sufficient amounts of food and not overfill their bodies with excessive calories. On the other side, the Western diet tricks our bodies into knowing their boundaries even longer than is ideal.

Chinese cuisine also supplements the food consumption by relying much on liquid foods. Western food is mostly dry, making it necessary for customers to drink water during the day. With daily consumption of Chinese food, there is no need for that, and desire would be better managed. You may know that Chinese food is good, but you do not know that it is one of the healthiest foods you can consume, either.

Healthy Carbohydrates

Carbohydrates give the organism the energy it needs to get through the day. They are converted to glycogen by the liver, a readily available resource in the muscles and liver.

Other types of energy resources, including fat, are unreliable. Good carbohydrates, including noodles and rice, are also used in Chinese meals, helping you remain energized without eating too many calories.

Nutritional Balance

It's essential to add carbohydrates, proteins, as well as other nutrients into your meal. Carbs supply the fuel required, while proteins help maintain and build muscle strength. That's why the ideal choice is Chinese food. Vegetables, noodles, or rice are often used in recipes, and any beef, fish, or other protein gives you a nutritious balance. It can be hard to find a meal that combines all these diverse nutritious elements into one dish with other cuisines.

Fiber

Fiber is another vital element, helping the body's digestive process. However, many individuals don't get plenty, so they don't like eating the soft vegetables that supply it. However, Chinese cuisine is remarkable for serving many well-seasoned and fried high-fiber dishes, giving them a more intense flavor.

Nutrition in Spices

Ginger- Ginger has a long history of use in traditional Chinese medicine; it has long been used to relieve vomiting and stimulate the appetite. Newer research has found that ginger can ease morning sickness and provoke pain that comes with osteoarthritis.

Garlic- Pungent garlic was used in traditional medicine to relieve respiratory problems. It has a range of proven health effects, including decreasing cholesterol and the risk of osteoporosis and some cancers, plus these have antibacterial activity.

Sesame Seeds- Sesame seeds are exploding with nutrients, including copper, iron, and calcium, and a heavy amount of fiber, although they are tiny.

Shiitake Mushrooms- Mushrooms add a pleasant aroma and taste to foods and make a perfect substitute for any or all of the meats in some sauces, allowing you to cut calories and maintain taste. A decent source of energy-producing Vitamin B and magnesium and immune-supporting manganese is shiitake mushrooms.

Tofu- Tofu is a perfect source to get a reasonable amount of protein from the vegetable resources. It is also an outstanding source of bone-building calcium and magnesium.

Bok Choy- This part of the cabbage family is rich in immune system-boosting vitamins A and C.

2.3 Specific Cooking Techniques Used in Chinese Restaurants

In China, there have been hundreds of ways of cooking. However, deep-frying, stir-frying, braising, shallow-frying, heating, boiling, and reheating are the most common techniques.

Stir-Frying

The most widely used process is stir-frying. This process cooks the manufactured ingredients for a brief amount of time at high temperatures. As the source of heating, edible oil is being used. Usually, a wok will be used at high temperatures, spices, and seasonings to apply edible oil. Owing to the brief amount of time involved with the process, foods mostly retain their nutrient benefit. Usually, stir-fried meat is moist and crispy, and vegetables are normally soft and crispy.

Deep Frying

Deep-frying requires much more vegetable oil than stir-frying (the component should be entirely immersed in the fat), providing buttery-textured food. The traditional way of making deep-frying dishes is to break the components into medium-sized parts or pieces, soak them in seasoned spices for a while, cover with corn flour and finally fry in warm cooking oil over medium-high heat. The coating thickness will decide the degree of crunchiness and gentleness on the inside and outside of the products used.

Shallow Frying

Shallow-frying is a preparation method requiring fewer oil products than used in deep-frying and less temperature than stir-frying. Shallow-fried foods are typically very delicate inside, becoming golden or mildly burnt externally. The products for shallow-frying are typically split into strips or flat pieces and brushed with herbs and spices. After being processed, the ingredients are also partially brushed with corn flour to make the external skin crispy. When frying, the products should be shallow-fried on one side first and then switched to the other.

Braising

To prepare large-sized foods crumble-in-your-mouth, braising is to add ingredients and flavorings in a wok or a frying pan simultaneously, add in some water, heat it, and then simmer it for an hour more than. The components are usually formed into pieces or stones. To fry dishes by braising, the seasoning mixes, especially the animal products, should be rid of the strange smell in boiling water and washed in clean water first. The sauce is thickened either with corn flour or reduced by simmering eventually.

Steaming

A special form of cooking developed in China is steaming. It is commonly used for steaming tortillas and wontons in northern China, where people survive on wheaten rice. The method involves putting the materials in a steamer basket, which is put over the liquid in a steamer jar. Steamed food provides more nutrients than that which is dissolved into the water for less protein. Quite little edible oil and fewer seasonings are used, so the food's natural taste is preserved and improved.

Roasting

Roasting is to prepare the food over the open fire of coal or in a microwave. Although seasonings are rubbed in from outside, the odor of the food is eliminated. The roast food's surface still gets denser and golden brown, but it preserves and improves flavors. Many products can be fried, like all meat types, just like most root and bulb veggies. To roast poultry, the products must be prepared, processed, and braised with edible oil to avoid moisture in the products during the roasting process.

Chapter 3: Chinese Appetizers and Breakfast Recipes

3.1 Delicious Chinese Appetizer Recipes

Chef John's Shrimp Toast

Cooking Time: 24 minutes

Serving Size: 4

Calories: 212.3

Ingredients:

- 1 tablespoon soy sauce
- 1 egg white
- ½ teaspoon white sugar
- ½ teaspoon paprika
- ½ pound raw shrimp
- ½ cup finely sliced green onions

- 3 garlic cloves
- Salt to taste
- 4 slices white bread
- 1 teaspoon sesame seeds
- 1 tablespoon ginger root
- 1 anchovy filet
- 1 teaspoon sesame oil
- ¼ cup cilantro leaves
- 1 teaspoon Asian fish sauce
- 1 pinch cayenne pepper
- 1 cup of vegetable oil

Method:

1. Blend all ingredients in a food processor and blend until the mixture becomes smooth.
2. Lightly toast slices of bread and paste shrimp mixture over toasts.
3. Cut edges and slice into halves.
4. Add vegetable oil in the skillet and fry until golden brown.
5. Serve hot with green onion.

Pork Dumplings

Cooking Time: 35 minutes

Serving Size: 100 dumplings

Calories: 751.5

Ingredients:

- 5 cups Chinese cabbage

- 100 wonton wrappers
- 1 ¾ pounds pork
- 1 tablespoon fresh ginger root
- 3 tablespoons sesame oil
- 4 cloves garlic
- 2 tablespoons green onion
- 4 tablespoons soy sauce
- 1 egg

Method:

1. In a bowl, combine the soy sauce, pork, sesame oil, green onion, ginger, garlic, egg, and cabbage.
2. Add 1 teaspoon cabbage mixture into each wonton wrapper and form a triangle shape.
3. Steam dumplings for 20 to 25 minutes and serve hot.

Chinese Chicken Wings

Cooking Time: 65 minutes

Serving Size: 12

Calories: 256.1

Ingredients:

- 2 tablespoons garlic powder
- 5 pounds of chicken wings
- 2 cups soy sauce
- 2 cups brown sugar

Method:

1. Mix all ingredients except chicken wings.
2. Heat ingredients until brown sugar melts completely.

3. Pour mixture over chicken wings and wrap the bowl with plastic cover.
4. Marinate chicken for 8 hours in the refrigerator.
5. Heat oven on 365°F.
6. Cover chicken with aluminum foil and bake for 45 minutes in the oven.
7. Remove foil and bake for 15 minutes more.
8. Serve hot with sauce.

Perfect Pot Stickers

Cooking Time: 30 minutes

Serving Size: 6

Calories: 438.5

Ingredients:

- ½ cup green onions
- 1 pinch cayenne pepper
- 1 ½ cups green cabbage
- 3 tablespoons fresh ginger
- 2 tablespoons soy sauce
- 1-pound pork
- 4 cloves garlic
- 1 teaspoon sesame oil

Dipping Sauce:

- ¼ cup of rice vinegar
- ¼ cup of soy sauce

Dough Ingredients:

- ¾ teaspoon kosher salt

- 2 ½ cups all-purpose flour
- 1 cup hot water

Frying:
- 8 tablespoons water for steaming
- 6 tablespoons vegetable oil

Method:
1. Mix green onion, cabbage, pepper, garlic, ginger soy sauce, sesame oil, and pork in a bowl and mix with a fork.
2. Cover with plastic and chill for an hour in the refrigerator.
3. Mix dough ingredients and make the dough.
4. Knead dough until it becomes soft and smooth.
5. Wrap the dough and let it rest for 30 minutes.
6. Cut dough into small pieces and make sticker wrappers.
7. Fill stickers with pork mixture and fold.
8. Mix dipping sauce ingredients to make the dipping sauce.
9. Heat a skillet and put pot stickers in hot oil until golden brown.
10. Drizzle water and steam for 7 minutes or until crispy.
11. Serve with dipping sauce.

Chinese Egg Rolls

Cooking Time: 70 minutes

Serving Size: 20

Calories: 169

Ingredients:
- 8-ounce bamboo shoots
- 1 cup wood ear mushroom
- 4 teaspoons vegetable oil
- 3 large eggs
- 1 teaspoon sugar
- 14-ounce egg roll wrappers
- 1 egg white
- 1-pound roasted pork
- 2 green onions
- 2 ½ teaspoons soy sauce
- 4 cups oil for frying
- 1 medium head cabbage
- ½ carrot
- 1 teaspoon salt

Method:
1. Heat the skillet and add 1 tablespoon oil.
2. Add beaten egg in oil and cook for 2 minutes on low heat.
3. Change side and cook for another 1 minute.
4. Set aside and let it cool and slice into thin strips.
5. Add vegetable oil in skillet and heat remaining ingredients until vegetables are fully cooked.
6. Add sliced egg in vegetables and refrigerate for 1 hour.
7. Take a plastic wrapper and put vegetable mixture.
8. Roll plastic sheet until top corners are sealed.

9. Cover with plastic to avoid drying.

Chinese cabbage Pork Dumplings

Cooking Time: 95 minutes

Serving Size: 10

Calories: 120

Ingredients:

- 1 teaspoon sugar
- 1 teaspoon salt
- 2 ½ cups all-purpose flour
- 1 tablespoon scallions
- ¼ teaspoon salt
- ¾ cup of water
- ½ pound cabbage
- 1 teaspoon rice cooking wine
- 1 tablespoon ginger
- 1-pound pork sirloin

Method:

1. Mix flour and salt.
2. Add water and make an elastic, smooth dough.
3. Rest it for 10 minutes.
4. Divide the dough into small 50 pieces and roll into a thin circle piece.
5. Mix other ingredients and process slowly until well combined.
6. Add the mixture on pieces and make dumplings.
7. Steam for 6 to 7 minutes until cooked.

Chinese-Style Chicken and Mushrooms

Cooking Time: 40 minutes

Serving Size: 4

Calories: 170

Ingredients:

- ½ teaspoon sugar
- 1 garlic clove
- 100 grams of mushrooms
- ½ cup of water
- soy sauce
- olive oil
- 400 grams of chicken
- 3 teaspoons cornstarch
- salt
- black pepper
- 2 teaspoons fresh ginger

Method:

1. Cook mushrooms on low heat in a skillet with olive oil.
2. Cut chicken into pieces and add other ingredients over it.
3. Mix and marinate for 15 minutes.
4. Cook chicken pieces in skillet and add cooked mushrooms.
5. Heat until well cooked.
6. Serve with sauce.

Hand-Pulled Chinese Noodles

Cooking Time: 90 minutes

Serving Size: 4

Calories: 560

Ingredients:

- 2 teaspoons chili oil
- ¼ cup of soy sauce
- black sesame seeds
- 1 Thai Chile
- 3 ½ cups all-purpose flour
- ½ teaspoon kosher salt
- 1 green onion
- 4 teaspoons toasted sesame oil

Method:

1. Mix flour and salt.
2. Add water and make the dough.
3. Rest the dough for 30 minutes and cut into small pieces.
4. Pull these pieces into thin sticks.
5. Boil this for 10 minutes and rest aside.
6. Heat the skillet and add other ingredients to cook.
7. Add hand-pulled noodles and cook for more 2 minutes.
8. Serve with sauces.

Crispy Sesame Tofu and Broccoli

Cooking Time: 55 minutes

Serving Size: 4

Calories: 370

Ingredients:

- ½ teaspoon salt
- ¼ teaspoon pepper
- 2 scallions
- ¾ pound broccoli florets
- 2 teaspoons sesame seeds
- 1 garlic clove
- 3 tablespoons light brown sugar
- 4 teaspoons rice vinegar
- ½ inch fresh ginger
- 1-pound extra-firm tofu
- 1/3 cup water
- 2 teaspoons cornstarch
- 1/3 cup tamari
- 1 tablespoon toasted sesame oil
- 1 tablespoon neutral oil

Method:

1. Take tofu and rinse with water.
2. Add broccoli in a pan and heat with little water until broccoli becomes green and crispy.
3. Make tamari sauce with tamari, garlic, ginger, and seasoning.
4. Mix other ingredients and cook on low heat.
5. Cut tofu into small pieces and put mixture with a spoon.

6. Heat tofu on low heat until crispy.
7. Heat sauce until bubble comes out.
8. Add broccoli and tofu into the bubbling sauce.
9. Mix for 2 minutes and serve with scallions on top.

Cream Cheese Wontons

Cooking Time: 30 minutes

Serving Size: 6

Calories: 228

Ingredients:

- 8 ounces cream cheese
- ½ teaspoon sugar
- 24 wonton wrappers
- 1 egg beaten
- oil for frying
- 2 teaspoons minced chives
- ½ teaspoon onion powder

Method:

1. Combine and mix sugar, cream cheese, and onion powder.
2. Place a wonton wrapper and put a teaspoon on cream cheese over it.
3. Brush edges with egg and wraps into package shape.
4. Heat pan on 350°F with 4 tablespoon oil.
5. Fry wontons for 6 to 7 minutes or until golden brown.
6. Soak into a paper towel and set aside.
7. Fry all wonton wraps and serve with tamari sauce.

Lumpia Shanghai

Cooking Time: 25 minutes

Serving Size: 6

Calories: 230

Ingredients:

- 3 cups cooking oil
- 50 pieces lumpia wrappers

Filling Ingredients:

- ½ teaspoon black pepper
- ½ cup parsley
- 1 ½ lb. ground pork
- 1 tablespoon sesame oil
- 2 eggs
- 2 pieces onion
- 1 ½ teaspoons salt
- 2 pieces of carrots
- 1 ½ teaspoon garlic powder

Method:

1. Mix all filling ingredients in a bowl and stir.
2. Take lumpia wrap and put fillings on it.
3. Beat an egg and brush it to edges.
4. Roll wrappers and set aside.
5. Heat the skillet with oil and put wrappers into the hot oil.
6. Cook until lumpia floats in oil.
7. Soak extra oil and serve with sauce.

3.2 Chinese Breakfast Recipes

Here are some breakfast recipes to start your day with delicious and easy Chinese dishes to save your energy for the whole day.

Chinese Pork Salad

Cooking Time: 10 minutes

Serving Size: 6

Calories: 124

Ingredients:

- ½ cup stir-fry sauce
- ½ red onion
- 3 ounces chow Mein noodles
- 20 ounces pea pods
- 8 ounces mandarin oranges
- 1-pound pork strips (stir-fry)

Method:

1. Marinate pork strips in the sauce for 25 minutes.
2. Stir-fry pork in a large skillet for 6 to 7 minutes.
3. Mix remaining ingredients in a bowl.
4. Mix pork sauce and mixture.
5. Stir and serve.

Chinese-Style Spareribs

Cooking Time: 2 hours

Serving Size: 6

Calories: 77

Ingredients:

- 3 tablespoons dry sherry
- 2 cloves garlic
- 6 pounds pork spareribs
- 2 tablespoons honey
- 2 tablespoons soy sauce
- ¼ cup hoisin sauce
- ¼ cup of water

Method:

1. Take spareribs and cut them into pieces.
2. Mix all ingredients in a bowl.
3. Take a large sealing bag and put ribs into it.
4. Take ¼ cup of mixture and rest aside.
5. Add the remaining mixture in the bag and mix well with ribs.
6. Marinate mixture in the refrigerator for 1 hour.
7. Heat oven at 350°F and take a baking pan.
8. Put ribs in pan and wrap with baking sheet to bake for 90 minutes.
9. Remove the sheet and put the remaining ¼ cup of mixture on the ribs with a brush.
10. Bake for another 30 minutes.
11. Serve hot with sauce.

Crunchy Chinese Pork Salad

Cooking Time: 20 minutes

Serving Size: 4

Calories: 141

Ingredients:

- 3 ounces chow Mein noodles
- 6 cups iceberg lettuce
- 4 slices bacon
- ½ cup green onions
- 3 tablespoons soy sauce
- 8 ounces water chestnuts
- ¾ pound roasted pork loin
- 1 tablespoon ketchup
- 2 tablespoons honey
- 1 teaspoon mustard

Method:

1. Cook bacon until crisp and set it aside.
2. Take a small bowl and stir ketchup, mustard, and soy sauce together.
3. Take a large bowl and mix pork, bacon, lettuce, green onions, and chestnut together.
4. Add noodles in dressing and salad.
5. Mix well and serve.

Chinese Tomato and Egg Sauté

Cooking Time: 30 minutes

Serving Size: 2

Calories: 810

Ingredients:
- 3 pinches shredded coconut
- black pepper
- 1 tablespoon ketchup
- 1 teaspoon sugar
- 1 cup white rice
- ½ teaspoon sesame oil
- 1 teaspoon cornstarch
- 2 scallions
- 1 heirloom tomato
- 1 tablespoon rice wine
- 2 cups of water
- 4 large eggs
- 1 pinch salt

Method:
1. Chop the scallion and slice tomatoes into very little pieces.
2. Put eggs into a bowl and add seasonings.
3. Add rice wine and beat eggs.
4. Heat wok and add 2 tablespoon oil.
5. Add eggs and scramble. Set aside
6. Heat wok and add 1 tablespoon oil.
7. Add tomatoes and scallions.
8. Stir fry and add seasonings.
9. Add 1 cup of water and cooked eggs.

10. Mix and cover for 2-3 minutes until tomatoes make the paste.
11. Heat until sauce thickens as your requirement.

Chinese Meat Filled Buns (Baozi)

Cooking Time: 1 hour 45 minutes

Serving Size: 16

Calories: 105

Ingredients:
- 3 tablespoons sugar
- 1 teaspoon salt
- 50 milliliters cold water
- 300 grams pork (or chicken)
- 1 teaspoon fresh ginger
- 3 cloves garlic
- 2 spring onion
- 1 tablespoon rice wine
- 1 teaspoon sugar
- 3 shiitake mushrooms
- 2 tablespoons soy sauce
- 1 tablespoon oyster sauce
- 400 grams flour
- 1 ½ teaspoons baking powder
- ½ teaspoon sesame oil
- 3 tablespoons pork lard
- 190 milliliters warm water

- 2 teaspoons yeast

Method:
1. Mix flour, baking powder, yeast, sugar, and salt.
2. Add melted lard and warm water to make the dough.
3. Rest it for 30 minutes and knead until smooth.
4. Take other ingredients and mix them in a processor.
5. Take the dough and cut it into small pieces.
6. Prepare pieces into a circle and put fillings.
7. Roll again in a bun shape and set aside for 30 minutes.
8. Steam buns on a greaseproof paper so that they do not stick with sides of the steamer.
9. Steam for 15 to 20 minutes until it looks shiny and feels like buns.
10. Serve with sauce and lettuce.

Shao Bing - Chinese Breakfast Flatbread

Cooking Time: 65 minutes

Serving Size: 4

Calories: 740

Ingredients:
- 2 teaspoons Sichuan peppercorn
- 1 teaspoon spices
- 1 teaspoon chicken
- ¼ teaspoon salt
- 300 grams plain flour
- 1 tablespoon Chinese cooking wine
- ½ teaspoon salt

- 3 tablespoons vegetable oil
- ¼ cup oil
- 1 tablespoon soy sauce
- 250 grams ground beef
- ¼ cup spring onion
- 2 teaspoons ground ginger
- ¼ cup chopped onion
- 2 teaspoons sesame oil
- ¼ cup chopped coriander
- 2 tablespoons spring onion
- 1 ½ tablespoons flour
- 2 teaspoons white pepper
- sesame seeds

Method:
1. Making Dough- mix flour, salt and sugar in a bowl and mix until lumpy. Add yeast, water, and oil. Knead the dough and cover with plastic wrap. Set aside for 30 minutes.
2. Making Oil Paste- take a small pan and heat oil. Add cake flour and mix until smooth. Continue cooking until aromatic. Let it cool.
3. Heat oven at 425°F.
4. Forming Bread- take dough and roll dough. Add oil paste with spatula and roll dough again. Cut into pieces of bread and add sesame seeds on each bread.
5. Bake breads for 12 to 15 minutes until golden brown.
6. Cut the sides and serve with sauce.

Yang Chow Fried Rice

Cooking Time: 25 minutes

Serving Size: 6

Calories: 120

Ingredients:

- 2 large eggs
- 4 cups day-old rice
- 1 teaspoon toasted sesame oil
- ½ teaspoon kosher salt
- ½ teaspoon chicken bouillon
- ½ pound Chinese BBQ pork
- 3 scallions
- ½ teaspoon white pepper
- 3 tablespoons vegetable oil
- ¼ pound shrimp
- 1 tablespoon soy sauce
- 2 tablespoons oyster sauce

Method:

1. Fry shrimps in 1 tablespoon cooking oil. Set aside.
2. Cook chicken bouillon and scallions until softened.
3. Put rice in a wok and make a hole in the center.
4. Add beaten egg and mix with the rice properly.
5. Add other ingredients and chicken mixture in a pan and stir fry to make a paste.
6. Add paste on top of the rice. Serve hot.

Soya Sauce Mushroom Chicken with Braised Eggs

Cooking Time: 105 minutes

Serving Size: 1

Calories: 118

Ingredients:
- 4 cloves garlic
- 1 teaspoon sesame oil
- 4 eggs
- 3 pieces of chicken thighs
- 150 milliliters chicken broth
- 3 pieces of rock sugar
- 1 tablespoon corn flour
- 3 slices ginger
- 1 tablespoon Chinese cooking wine
- potato
- 6 button mushrooms
- 2-star anise
- 3 tablespoons light soy sauce
- 2 tablespoons dark soy sauce
- 1 dash pepper
- 1 cinnamon stick

Method:
1. Rinse chicken and dry with a towel.
2. Clean mushrooms and marinate chicken for 30 minutes.
3. Soak mushrooms for an hour.

4. Heat oil and add ginger, garlic, anise, cinnamon sticks.
5. Add chicken and stir fry for 5 minutes.
6. Add mushrooms and cook with the chicken for 10 minutes.
7. Add all other veggies and stir.
8. Cook on low heat for more than 20 minutes and add other ingredients.
9. Add corn flour to give thickness to the sauce and serve hot.

Chicken Mustard Green Congee – Chinese Breakfast Rice Porridge

Cooking Time: 55 minutes

Serving Size: 6

Calories: 190

Ingredients:

- ¼ cup mustard greens
- 1 tablespoon sesame oil
- 2 garlic cloves
- ¼ cup chives
- 12 ounces chicken tenderloin
- 1 ginger
- ¾ cup sweet rice
- ½ teaspoon dark soy sauce

Method:
1. Boil ginger, garlic on low heat in a pot, and add chicken.
2. Cook for 20 minutes until chicken cooked properly.
3. Shred chicken and discard ginger garlic.
4. Add rice in chicken broth water and cook for 25 minutes.
5. Add other ingredients and cook for more 5 minutes.
6. Rest aside for 10 minutes and serve.

Loaded Breakfast Baked Potatoes

Cooking Time: 80 minutes

Serving Size: 4

Calories: 470

Ingredients:
- 4 russet potatoes
- teaspoons salt
- teaspoons black pepper
- 2 scallions
- 1 tablespoon butter
- 4 large eggs
- 4 strips bacon
- 2 ounces cheddar cheese
- ½ teaspoon salt
- ¼ teaspoon black pepper
- sour cream
- hot sauce

Method:
1. Heat the oven at 400°F and take an aluminum foil.
2. Pierce potatoes with fork and place on aluminum foil sheet.
3. Bake potatoes for 60 to 70 minutes in the oven.
4. Take the potato and cut lengthwise with a knife to add fillings.
5. Heat the skillet and add other ingredients.
6. Stir until cooked.
7. Add mixture into potatoes and bake again for 10 minutes.
8. Serve immediately.

Baked Hash Brown Cups with Eggs

Cooking Time: 27 minutes

Serving Size: 4

Calories: 420

Ingredients:
- ½ cup shredded cheddar cheese
- chives
- ¼ teaspoon black pepper
- canola oil cooking spray
- 8 large eggs
- canola oil cooking spray
- 1 bag hash brown potatoes
- black pepper
- 4 strips bacon

- ½ teaspoon garlic powder
- salt

Method:
1. Heat oven at 400°F.
2. Place shredded potatoes in a bowl and mix with seasonings.
3. Press potatoes until water leaves.
4. Bake potatoes in muffin cups for 20 to 25 minutes.
5. Heat skillet and add beaten eggs.
6. Stir with a rubber spatula. Do not overcook eggs.
7. Add eggs and seasoning on potato and bake again for 3 to 7 minutes until fully melted.
8. Serve with sauce.

Steamed Halibut Fillet with Ginger and Scallions

Cooking Time: 45 minutes

Serving Size: 4

Calories: 500

Ingredients:
- 3 scallions
- 2 tablespoons canola oil
- 4 tablespoons water
- 2 inches fresh ginger
- 1 tablespoon chicken powder
- 2 ½ pounds fillets
- ¼ teaspoon salt
- 2 teaspoons sugar

- 4 baby bok choy
- vegetable oil cooking spray
- 3 tablespoons lite soy sauce
- 4 Chinese black mushrooms
- ¼ teaspoon black pepper

Method:
1. Mix all ingredients in a processor and mix until lightly smooth.
2. Add eggs and blend again.
3. Steam fish fillets and place a lemon slice on each fillet.
4. Bring to boil water and steam for 3 to 4 minutes after the water starts boiling. Do not overcook.
5. Place fillets in a dish and pour the sauce over it. Cool at room temperature. Serve with spinach leaves.

Chapter 4: Chinese Lunch and Snack Recipes

4.1 Chinese Snack Recipes

Seasoned Snack Mix

Cooking Time: 30 minutes

Serving Size: 10

Calories: 450

Ingredients:

- ¼ cup Crisco Butter Flavor
- ¾ teaspoon garlic salt
- ¼ teaspoon cayenne pepper
- 2 cups oyster crackers
- 7 ounces peanuts
- ¾ cup grated Parmesan cheese
- salt

- ¼ teaspoon onion powder
- 3 cups of rice
- 2 teaspoons Worcestershire sauce
- 2 teaspoons Italian seasoning
- 1 square cereal
- 2 cups round toasted oat cereal
- 2 cups pretzel sticks

Method:
1. Preheat oven at 325°F.
2. Melt shortening in the oven and rest it aside.
3. Add Worcestershire sauce, seasoning, garlic, ginger, salt, and pepper in a bowl and stir.
4. Add other ingredients and melted shortenings into the mixture.
5. Mix well and spread evenly on the baking sheet.
6. Bake 16 to 18 minutes in oven and stir after 10 minutes.
7. Cool and store in containers.

Energy Snack Cake

Cooking Time: 85 minutes

Serving Size: 4

Calories: 920

Ingredients:
- 300 grams walnut pieces
- 100 grams flour
- 60 grams of dried cranberries
- 10 dried figs

- ½ teaspoon baking soda
- ¼ teaspoon baking powder
- 3 large eggs
- 15 grams of dried dates
- 80 grams of dried apricots
- ½ teaspoon salt
- 140 grams of sugar
- 1 teaspoon vanilla extract

Method:
1. Mix baking powder, baking soda, flour, and salt in a bowl.
2. Add nuts, dried fruits, and sugar in the mixture.
3. Heat oven to 150°F.
4. Take a small bowl and beat eggs with vanilla extract.
5. Add egg mixture into the flour mixture and mix well.
6. Add other ingredients and pour them into a baking pan.
7. Bake for 60 to 70 minutes.
8. Let it cool and cut into slices.

Taco Snack Mix

Cooking Time: 16 minutes

Serving Size: 4

Calories: 120

Ingredients:
- 2 cups crackers
- 2 cups of corn chips

- 2 cups Rice Chex Cereal
- 1 package McCormick Taco Seasoning Mix
- 2 cups Wheat Chex Cereal
- ½ cup unsalted butter

Method:
1. Microwave butter for 40 seconds until butter melts.
2. Take a bowl and mix cereals, corn chips, cheese crackers.
3. Add seasoning in the mixture and stir well.
4. Microwave mixture uncovered for 6 to 8 minutes until crispy.
5. Cool at room temperature.

One-Bowl Caramel Snack Cake with Caramel Glaze

Cooking Time: 60 minutes

Serving Size: 9

Calories: 610

Ingredients:
- ¾ cup cake flour
- 1 ½ teaspoons baking powder
- ¼ cup confectioners' sugar
- 1 large egg
- 2 large egg yolks
- cooking oil spray
- ¾ cup unsalted butter
- ¾ teaspoon salt

For cake:

- 1 cup dark brown sugar
- 1 cup heavy cream
- 1 tablespoon vanilla extract
- 1 cup all-purpose flour

For caramel:

- ½ cup heavy cream
- 1 teaspoon flaky sea salt
- 1 teaspoon vanilla extract
- 1 cup dark brown sugar

Method:

1. Heat oven at 350°F and Grease the pan with oil. Set aside.
2. Melt butter in the microwave oven and separate ¼ cup.
3. Add brown sugar and cream in remaining butter.
4. Microwave 1 minute and stir. Microwave for more 1 minute until caramel thickens. Set aside to cool down.
5. Use powder ingredients and mix them into the caramel.
6. Stir with a rubber spatula until combine.
7. Bake for 20 minutes on the middle rack.
8. Rotate baking pan and bake for more than 20 minutes until softens.
9. Pour remaining butter and caramel on the cake and set aside.
10. Let it cool down for 10 minutes and cut into pieces.

Snack Dippers with Hillshire Farm Smoked Sausage and Honey Mustard

Cooking Time: 35 minutes

Serving Size: 10

Calories: 170

Ingredients:

- 2 tablespoons yellow mustard
- 1 tablespoon honey
- ¼ cup packed brown sugar
- ¼ cup mayonnaise
- ¼ teaspoon black pepper
- 14 ounces Smoked Sausage

Method:

1. Place sausages in a tray and unwrap. Freeze for 30 minutes.
2. Use a cutting board to cut sausages into ¼ size pieces.
3. Heat oven to 325°F.
4. Transfer sausages in the baking dish and spread brown sugar.
5. Bake sausages for 20 minutes until lightly browned.
6. Mix other ingredients in a bowl and dip sausages to serve.

Afternoon Snack Muffins

Cooking Time: 65 minutes

Serving Size: 4

Calories: 760

Ingredients:

- 4 eggs
- 2 tablespoons chocolate sprinkles
- 1 container yogurt
- 200 grams flour
- 100 grams margarine
- 200 grams of sugar
- 1 teaspoon baking powder
- 1 handful walnuts

Method:

1. Heat oven to 180°C.
2. Grease muffin pan with butter and flour. Set aside.
3. Beat sugar and eggs until the mixture becomes fluffy.
4. Add yogurt and margarine. Beat again.
5. Add baking powder and flour. Beat again until it forms a smooth batter.
6. Add chocolate sprinkles and walnuts. Stir with a spoon.
7. Place dough in muffin cups and bake for 50 minutes.
8. Remove from the oven and let it cool down.

Wheat Bread Snack

Cooking Time: 10 minutes

Serving Size: 4

Calories: 90

Ingredients:

- watercress

- 1 slice whole-wheat bread
- olive oil
- 1 cup skimmed milk

Method:

1. Toast bread to a golden-brown color.
2. Pour watercress and olive oil on toast.
3. Serve with milk.

Apple Peanut Butter Snack

Cooking Time: 10 minutes

Serving Size: 2

Calories: 360

Ingredients:

- 2 tablespoons sunflower kernels
- ¼ cup Smucker's Peanut Butter
- 2 apples
- ¼ teaspoon ground cinnamon
- ¼ cup plain yogurt
- 1 tablespoon apple juice

Method:

1. Cut the apple into small slices.
2. Mix cinnamon, yogurt, peanut butter, apple juice, and kernels in processor and blend well.
3. Apply mixture evenly on sliced apples and let it cool down.

Honey Almond Snack Mix

Cooking Time: 15 minutes

Serving Size: 4

Calories: 320

Ingredients:

- 2 cups of cereal
- 2 cups of rice cereal squares
- 1 cup whole almonds
- ½ teaspoon salt
- ½ teaspoon ground red pepper
- ¼ cup Coconut Oil
- ¼ cup honey

Method:

1. Heat oven to 365°F.
2. Grease pan with baking paper and flour. Set aside.
3. Combine almonds, salt, pepper, and cereals in large bowls.
4. Take a small bowl and mix honey with coconut.
5. Pour in cereal mixture and stir well.
6. Spread into baking pan and bake for 15 to 18 minutes.
7. Let it cool and cut into slices.

Chinese BBQ Pork

Cooking Time: 20 minutes

Serving Size: 4

Calories: 352

Ingredients:

- 1 tablespoon honey
- 2 teaspoons fresh ginger root
- ½ cup dry sherry
- 8 drops red food coloring
- 2 pounds pork loin roast
- 1 teaspoon sesame oil
- 1 whole scallion
- 3 tablespoons soy sauce
- 2 ½ tablespoons hoisin sauce

Method:

1. Cut pork into small pieces.
2. Take a cooking bowl and grease with oil.
3. Place all ingredients in the cooker and mix.
4. Cover and cook for 7 hours on low heat.
5. Serve with fried rice.

Yam Bean, Carrot, and Cucumber Snack

Cooking Time: 45 minutes

Serving Size: 3

Calories: 260

Ingredients:

- Worcestershire sauce
- Peanuts
- 2 carrots
- ½ yam bean

- Unflavored gelatin
- Hot sauce
- Lime juice
- Japanese peanuts
- 1 cucumber
- 6 limes

Method:
1. Grate carrot, yam beans, and cucumber. Drain all thoroughly.
2. Grease baking pan with oil and pour beans.
3. Sprinkle gelatin and lime slices. Press firmly.
4. Add a layer of cucumber and carrots with the same process.
5. Cover and freeze for 30 minutes.
6. Mix other ingredients to make the sauce.
7. Sprinkle peanuts for garnish.

4.2 Chinese Lunch Recipes

These are some Chinese recipes that are common in the Chinese menu and easy to prepare with fewer ingredients.

Stir-Fried Tofu with Rice

Cooking Time: 40 minutes

Serving Size: 2

Calories: 281

Ingredients:

For the Tofu:

- 100 grams of tofu
- 1-inch ginger
- 3 Garlic cloves
- 1-inch red onion
- 1 Lemongrass stick
- 2 Shallots
- A handful of coriander leaves
- 1 teaspoon refined oil
- 2 teaspoon soya sauce

- 2 teaspoon chili paste
- 2 teaspoon honey

For the Fried Rice:

- 2 teaspoon soya sauce
- ½ Lemon
- Carrots
- Coriander leaves
- 1 teaspoon olive oil
- Spring onions
- Salt and pepper
- 1 Fresh red chilly
- 1 Ginger

Method:

1. Add chopped mariner in a preheated pan and stir well.
2. Add seasonings, garlic, shallots, and ginger.
3. Add honey, soy sauce, and chili paste.
4. Add coriander and mix with a rubber spatula. Set aside.
5. Mix carrot, onion, salt, pepper, and ginger in a pan.
6. Drizzle in oil then add chili, lemon juice, and soy sauce.
7. Add coriander in cooked rice and cook for 7 more minutes.
8. Serve rice.

Dim Sums

Cooking Time: 1 hour 20 minutes

Serving Size: 4

Calories: 237

Ingredients:

For Chicken and Prawn Dumplings:

- 5 ml sesame oil
- 2.5 grams white pepper
- 150 grams of chicken
- Wonton skin
- Potato starch
- 150 grams prawn
- 5 grams of sugar
- Salt

For Vegetable Coriander Dumplings:

- 10 grams of water chestnuts
- 10 grams of carrots
- 10 grams button mushrooms
- 5 grams of sugar
- 10 grams garlic
- 10 grams of bamboo shoots
- 5 grams sesame oil
- 10 ml of oil
- 10 grams brown garlic

For Wonton Skin:

- Salt
- 50 grams of wheat starch
- Potato starch

Method:
1. Mix prawns and chicken with salt, potato starch, sesame oil, and sugar.
2. Stuff wanton skin in mixture and steam. Serve with soya sauce.
3. For dumplings, mix all ingredients except wanton skin.
4. Stuff mixture in wanton skin and steam. Serve with sauce.
5. To prepare wanton skin, add potato in wheat starch, salt, and water.
6. Add potato starch and stir till tightens.
7. Cut into pieces and roll balls. Add fillings.
8. For the sauce, fry garlic in oil. Soak chilies and make a paste.
9. Add chili paste when garlic gets brown. Add seasonings.

Hot and Sour Soup

Cooking Time: 1 hour 15 minutes

Serving Size: 4

Calories: 39

Ingredients:
- 1 ½ tablespoon vinegar
- Salt
- 60 grams prawns
- 1 tablespoon soya sauce
- ½ tablespoon chili powder
- 5 grams of carrot

- 5 grams of cabbage
- 1 Egg
- 1 tablespoon coriander
- 1 teaspoon chili oil
- 5 grams of bamboo shoots
- 5 grams black mushrooms
- 5 grams button mushrooms
- 100 grams of chicken
- ½ teaspoon white pepper
- 2 tablespoon corn flour
- 5 grams of bean sprouts
- 5 grams of fresh beans
- 2 cups stock

Method:

1. Cut all vegetables, prawns, and chickens into small pieces.
2. Cook all vegetables with chicken in a wok.
3. Add seasonings and other remaining ingredients into wok.
4. Add corn flour and egg in the end to a thick soup.

Quick Noodles

Cooking Time: 45 minutes

Serving Size: 2

Calories: 188

Ingredients:

- 1 cup carrot, julienne

- 1 tablespoon vegetable oil
- 1 cup onion
- 1 cup spring onions
- 2 packets noodles
- 1 tablespoon ginger and garlic chili paste
- 1 tablespoon coriander
- 1 tablespoon lemon juice
- 1 teaspoon vinegar
- 1 tablespoon soy sauce
- 1 tablespoon Schezuan sauce
- 1 cup pepper
- 1 cup mushrooms
- ½ lettuce
- ½ teaspoon turmeric powder
- 1 teaspoon sugar

Method:
1. Cook noodles using instructions on the pack. Drain and cool in the water.
2. Add oil in noodles and mix to avoid sticking noodles with each other.
3. Heat oil in a wok.
4. Mix vegetables and soya sauce, mushroom, ginger, and garlic paste and fry in wok.
5. Mix remaining ingredients in a small bowl and stir.
6. Add this mixture to vegetable mixture and add noodles. Mix well.

7. Garnish with chopped coriander and serve.

Szechuan Chili Chicken

Cooking Time: 45 minutes

Serving Size: 8

Calories: 179

Ingredients:

- 3 tablespoon brown peppercorn
- Salt
- 2-3 spring onions
- 2 teaspoon white pepper
- 5-6 dry red chilies
- 2-3 tablespoon ginger
- 3 tablespoon green peppercorn
- 10-12 pieces chicken
- 1 tablespoon black vinegar
- 2 teaspoon chili oil
- oil for frying

Method:

1. Fry chicken with ginger until color changes to brown.
2. Drain oil and set it aside.
3. Add onion, garlic, peppercorn, and brown peppercorn.
4. Sauté for 5 minutes and add spices.
5. Stir for more than 10 minutes and add black vinegar.
6. Fry for more than 10 minutes and garnish with peppercorns.

Shitake Fried Rice with Water Chestnuts

Cooking Time: 25 minutes

Serving Size: 2

Calories: 291

Ingredients:

- 1 Cup Shitake mushroom
- 1 tablespoon Ginger
- A pinch of White pepper
- 1 big drop Sesame oil
- 1 cup rice (cooked)
- Green chilies
- 2-3 tablespoon Vegetable oil
- 4 cloves garlic
- 2-3 Water chestnuts
- 1 big tablespoon Celery
- ½ Medium Onion
- 1 big tablespoon Leeks
- Small bunch Parsley
- A dash of Rice wine vinegar
- 1 big drop of Sesame oil
- Salt to season
- 1 stalk Spring onions

Method:

1. Slice mushrooms, chestnuts, and green chilies.
2. Heat wok and add 1 tablespoon vegetable oil.

3. Add celery, onion, and leeks in oil.
4. Add mushrooms, chestnuts, and ginger.
5. Add rice, onion, sauces, and other ingredients.
6. Stir fry and put into the bowl.

Chicken with Chestnuts

Cooking Time: 45 minutes

Serving Size: 4

Calories: 294

Ingredients:

- 5 dried Chinese mushrooms
- 1 tablespoon fish sauce
- 1 tablespoon date puree
- 1 diced green capsicum
- 2 tablespoon sesame oil
- ½ kg chicken mince
- 1 diced red capsicum
- 3 tablespoon white radish
- 50 ml of water
- ½ teaspoon chili flakes
- 12-14 peeled water chestnuts
- 2 tablespoon chopped spring onion
- 1 tablespoon chopped garlic
- 1 tablespoon vinegar
- 1 iceberg lettuce
- 1 tablespoon shredded ginger

- 1 tablespoon soya sauce
- 1 tablespoon chopped coriander

Method:
1. Soak mushrooms in boiling water for 30 minutes and discard stems of mushrooms.
2. Heat oil in wok and fry chicken with ginger until lightly browned.
3. Fry ginger, garlic, and capsicum for 3 minutes.
4. Put the chicken into pan and heat.
5. Add remaining ingredients into chicken except for lettuce and coriander.
6. Add vegetables and mix well.
7. Serve with lettuce and garnish with coriander leaves.

Honey Chili Potato

Cooking Time: 35 minutes

Serving Size: 2

Calories: 586

Ingredients:

For Frying Potatoes:
- 5 tablespoon Corn flour
- 2 Potatoes
- 1 ½ tablespoon Salt
- 2 teaspoon Chili Powder

For Honey Chili Sauce:
- 4 teaspoon Sesame Seeds
- 2 tablespoon Honey

- 1 teaspoon Chili Flakes
- 2 Bulbs Spring Onions
- 1 ½ teaspoon Garlic
- 1 teaspoon Vinegar
- 2 teaspoon Tomato Sauce
- 2 teaspoon Chili Sauce
- 1 teaspoon Ginger
- 2 Whole Red Chilies
- 1 teaspoon salt

Method:

1. Take 2 potatoes and cut them into lengthwise slices.
2. Rinse them with water and soak for 15 minutes.
3. Add slices into a bowl and put some salt, corn flour, chili, and coriander leaves.
4. Mix well until sticky.
5. Take a frying pan and heat 3 tablespoon oil.
6. Fry potatoes into the oil until golden brown and crispy.
7. Do not fry on high flame as it can cause potatoes to burn from the outer side and uncooked from the inner side.
8. When cooked properly, set aside.
9. Take another frying pan and put sesame seeds to heat until golden brown. Set aside.
10. Heat oil in a pan and add chili flakes, tomato sauce, ginger, garlic, and red chilies.
11. Stir well and add vinegar, chili sauce, honey, and salt.
12. Stir and make the sauce.

13. Add fried potatoes in sauce and mix well.
14. Serve potatoes with juice.

Peri-Peri Chicken Satay

Cooking Time: 25 minutes

Serving Size: 2

Calories: 104

Ingredients:

- 50 grams Peri-Peri sauce
- 100 grams of potato fries
- 100 grams of yogurt
- 200 grams of chicken thigh
- salt and pepper
- 5 grams of chili powder
- Oil to fry
- 25 grams ginger garlic paste
- 5 grams coriander leaves

Method:

1. Soak skewers for 60 minutes.
2. Add ginger, garlic, salt, pepper, Peri-Peri sauce, chili, and garlic in a bowl.
3. Mix well and add chicken.
4. Marinate for 2 hours in a sealing bag.
5. Heat grill on medium heat.
6. Place chicken on grill and brush with oil to prevent sticking.
7. Grill for 15 to 20 minutes until brown.

8. Serve chicken with crispy potato fries.

Cantonese Chicken Soup

Cooking Time: 40 minutes

Serving Size: 2

Calories: 132

Ingredients:

- 5 spoons large chicken stock
- 10 Mushrooms
- 1 whole chicken
- 5 Pieces bok choy
- 3-4 spring onions

Method:

1. Cut chicken skin and piece chicken into large slices about 10 to 12.
2. Cut mushrooms into halves.
3. Take a container and layer bok choy, mushrooms, and chicken evenly.
4. Add chicken stock and cook for an hour.
5. Add remaining ingredients and water as your requirement.
6. Cook for more than 20 minutes.
7. Use corn flour to give thickness to the soup.

Vegetable Manchow Soup

Cooking Time: 35 minutes

Serving Size: 2

Calories: 128.8

Ingredients:
- 2 tablespoon French beans
- 2 tablespoon Carrots
- 2 Spring onions
- 1 teaspoon Pepper
- 4 Cups Water
- 2 tablespoon Mushrooms
- 1 teaspoon Ginger
- 1 teaspoon Garlic
- 1 teaspoon Green chilies
- 2 stems Spring onion
- Oil and salt
- 1 tablespoon Coriander leaves
- 2 tablespoon Cabbage
- 1 tablespoon Soya sauce
- 4 tablespoon Corn flour
- 1 cup Water
- 2 tablespoon Capsicum

Method:
1. Stir fry coriander leaves, garlic, green chilies, and ginger for 2 minutes.
2. Cut all vegetables and add them into the ginger-garlic mixture.
3. Add seasonings and sauces. Fry for more than 5 minutes.
4. Add water and wait until it starts boiling.

5. Take a small bowl and mix corn flour in hot water.
6. Add corn flour mixture into boiling water and vegetable mixture.
7. Stir until it starts thickening.
8. Remove from heat and garnish with green onions.

Garlic Soya Chicken

Cooking Time: 35 minutes

Serving Size: 2

Calories: 119.3

Ingredients:

- ¼ teaspoon White Pepper
- 1 teaspoon Ginger Juice
- 450 Gram Chicken Breast
- 1 teaspoon Sesame Oil
- 1 tablespoon ginger, grated
- 1 tablespoon Rice Vinegar
- 2 tablespoon Vegetable oil
- A handful of Snow Peas
- 2 tablespoon Soy Sauce
- 5-6 Garlic cloves
- ½ Cup Red Onion
- 1 teaspoon Red Chili Flakes
- ½ Red Bell Pepper

For the Sauce:

- 2 teaspoon Chinese Rice Wine

- ½ tablespoon Brown Sugar
- 1 teaspoon Corn flour
- 2 teaspoon Dark Soy Sauce

Method:
1. Cut chicken into small pieces.
2. Take a large bowl and mix chicken with sesame oil and white pepper.
3. Marinate chicken for 15 to 20 minutes.
4. Take a small bowl and mix all ingredients of sauces and mix well.
5. Put a frying pan on low heat. Add 2 tablespoon oil and spread it into a frying pan.
6. Gradually add chicken pieces into the frying pan and wait for 5 minutes.
7. The flame should be low. Wait until chicken sides turn into light brown color.
8. Stir chicken until all sides turn brown and remove immediately from the frying pan.
9. Turn the heat up and fry peas and red onion for 1 minute.
10. Stir continuously to prevent burning or overheating.
11. Add bell pepper and cook for one more minute.
12. Mix all ingredients well and when vegetables get crispy, stir in chicken.
13. Make sauce ingredients and cook on low heat until sticky and smooth.
14. Pour sauce on chicken and vegetables.

15. Add 1 tablespoon water and cook for 2 minutes until bubbly and thick.
16. Serve with fried rice and lettuce.

Chapter 5: Chinese Dinner and Dessert Recipes

5.1 Dinner Recipes of Chinese Cuisine

Shrimp Fried Rice

Cooking Time: 20 minutes

Serving Size: 6

Calories: 332

Ingredients:

- 1 package frozen mixed vegetables
- 1-pound medium shrimp
- 4 tablespoons butter
- 4 large eggs
- ¼ teaspoon pepper
- 8 bacon strips

- 3 cups cold cooked rice
- ½ teaspoon salt

Method:
1. Take a large skillet and heat on low flame.
2. Add 1 tablespoon vegetable oil or butter.
3. Beat eggs and pour into skillet.
4. Stir to cook on all sides. Remove from skillet and set aside.
5. Melt butter in the skillet again and add vinegar.
6. Add cooked rice and shrimp into the skillet.
7. Stir and cook for 5 minutes until shrimp color changes to pink.
8. Cut eggs into pieces and add in skillet. Cook on low flame.
9. Remove from flame after 5 minutes and garnish with coriander leaves.

Ginger-Cashew Chicken Salad

Cooking Time: 30 minutes

Serving Size: 8

Calories: 379

Ingredients:
- ¼ teaspoon cayenne pepper
- 4 boneless skinless chicken breast halves
- ½ cup cider vinegar
- 2 teaspoons reduced-sodium soy sauce
- 1 teaspoon salt

- ½ cup molasses
- ½ cup canola oil
- 2 tablespoons minced fresh gingerroot

For Salad:
- 2 tablespoons sesame seeds
- 1 can mandarin oranges
- 1 cup shredded red cabbage
- 3 green onions
- 2 cups Chow Mein noodles
- 8 ounces fresh baby spinach
- ¾ cup salted cashews
- 2 medium carrots

Method:
1. Blend all ingredients in a processor except chicken.
2. Add chicken in a bowl and pour processed ingredients over it.
3. Mix and marinate chicken for 3 hours.
4. Heat the broiler and put the chicken into it.
5. Boil for 20 minutes. Change sides and boil for 15 more minutes.
6. Cut the ingredients of salad and make noodles.
7. Add chicken in a separate dish, add salad and noodles. Serve with sauce.

Beef and Spinach Lo Mein

Cooking Time: 30 minutes

Serving Size: 5

Calories: 363

Ingredients:
- 1 tablespoon water
- 4 teaspoons canola oil
- 1 can sliced water chestnuts
- ¼ cup hoisin sauce
- 2 tablespoons soy sauce
- 1-pound beef top round steak
- 1 package fresh spinach
- 1 red chili pepper
- 6 ounces Spaghetti
- 2 teaspoons sesame oil
- 2 garlic cloves
- ¼ teaspoon crushed red pepper flakes
- 2 green onions

Method:
1. Mix hoisin, soy sauce, garlic, pepper, sesame oil, and water.
2. Separate ¼ cup of mixture in a large bowl.
3. Add beef in this mixture and mix well. Marinate for 10 minutes at room temperature.
4. Prepare spaghetti and follow package directions.
5. Take a skillet and heat it. Add canola oil.
6. Add the beef mixture in parts. Do not load the skillet with the whole mix.

7. Stir-fry beef mixture until pink. Remove and repeat with remaining mixture.
8. Heat a skillet and add remaining ingredients and hoisin mixture.
9. Cook for 15 minutes. Add beef mixture.
10. Add spaghetti and mix well. Cook for 5 minutes and serve hot.

Ginger Pork Lettuce Wraps

Cooking Time: 30 minutes

Serving Size: 2 dozen

Calories: 54

Ingredients:

- 1 tablespoon sesame oil
- 24 Boston lettuce leaves
- 1-pound lean ground pork
- 1 can sliced water chestnuts
- 4 green onions
- 1 medium onion
- ¼ cup hoisin sauce
- 1 tablespoon red wine vinegar
- 1 tablespoon reduced-sodium soy sauce
- 2 teaspoons Thai chili sauce
- 4 garlic cloves
- 1 tablespoon fresh ginger root

Method:
1. Take a large skillet and cook onion with pork for 10 minutes.
2. Remove when the pink color disappears, and onions become tender.
3. Cut into pieces and make crumbles.
4. Blend soy sauce, vinegar, garlic, ginger, and hoisin sauce.
5. Add remaining ingredients and heat for 10 minutes.
6. Place pork on lettuce leaves and mixture over it. Fold and serve.

Mushroom Pepper Steak

Cooking Time: 30 minutes

Serving Size: 4

Calories: 241

Ingredients:
- 1 cup julienned green pepper
- ½ teaspoon minced fresh ginger root
- 1-pound beef top sirloin steak
- 2 medium tomatoes
- 2 cups sliced fresh mushrooms
- 3 teaspoons canola oil
- 1 cup julienned sweet red pepper
- 6 tablespoons reduced-sodium soy sauce
- ¼ teaspoon pepper
- 1 garlic clove

- 6 green onions
- Hot cooked rice
- 1 tablespoon cornstarch
- ½ cup reduced-sodium beef broth

Method:
1. Take a bowl and mix salt, vinegar.
2. Add beef and mix well.
3. Marinate in the refrigerator for 30 to 60 minutes.
4. Take a small bowl and mix corn starch, soy sauce, and remaining broth.
5. Mix until smooth. Set aside.
6. Heat a skillet and add ginger, garlic in vegetable oil.
7. Add beef and discard the remaining marinade.
8. Stir fry beef in oil until no longer pink.
9. Remove from heat and set aside. Keep warm.
10. Stir fry mushrooms, vegetables with remaining ingredients and broth.
11. Add beef and mix well.
12. Cook for 10 minutes and serve with rice.

Asparagus Beef Sauté

Cooking Time: 30 minutes

Serving Size: 4

Calories: 328

Ingredients:
- 1-pound fresh asparagus
- 1 tablespoon canola oil

- 2 garlic cloves
- 1 green onion
- ½ teaspoon salt
- 1 ½ teaspoon lemon juice
- Hot cooked rice
- ½ pound sliced fresh mushrooms
- 1-pound beef tenderloin (¾ -inch cubes)
- ¼ teaspoon pepper
- ¼ cup butter
- 1 tablespoon reduced-sodium soy sauce

Method:
1. Mix salt and pepper with beef.
2. Take a frying pan and add 1 tablespoon cooking oil into it.
3. Add garlic and ginger. Stir fry for 2 minutes.
4. Add beef and fry for 10 minutes until lightly brown.
5. Remove from pan and set aside. Keep warm.
6. Add 1 tablespoon oil in the same skillet and put mushrooms.
7. Add asparagus and cook until tender. Add remaining ingredients and cook for 10 more minutes.
8. Add beef. Heat for 2 minutes and remove. Set aside and serve with rice.

Beef Orange Stir-Fry

Cooking Time: 25 minutes

Serving Size: 2

Calories: 390

Ingredients:

- ¼ cup of orange juice
- 2 teaspoons oil
- 3 cups vegetable (stir-fry)
- 1 tablespoon cornstarch
- 1 tablespoon soy sauce
- 1 garlic clove
- 1 cup hot cooked rice
- ½ pound beef sirloin steak
- ½ teaspoon sesame oil
- red flakes (pepper)
- ¼ cup of cold water

Method:

1. Take a small bowl and combine cornstarch, water, orange juice, soy sauce, pepper flakes, and sesame oil.
2. Stir until smooth. Set aside.
3. Heat wok and add 1 tablespoon vegetable oil. Add beef and heat.
4. Stir fry until golden brown.
5. Stir fry vegetables and cornstarch mixture in a skillet.
6. Add beef and other ingredients. Cook for 2 minutes and serve with rice.

Speedy Salmon Stir-Fry

Cooking Time: 30 minutes

Serving Size: 4

Calories: 498

Ingredients:

- 1 package frozen stir-fry vegetable blend
- 1 tablespoon molasses
- 1 tablespoon reduced-sodium soy sauce
- 1-pound salmon fillets
- 1 teaspoon grated orange zest
- 4 teaspoons canola oil
- 2 cups hot cooked brown rice
- 1 tablespoon sesame seeds
- 1 tablespoon minced fresh ginger root
- ¼ cup reduced-fat honey mustard salad dressing
- 2 tablespoons orange juice

Method:

1. Take a small bowl and mix honey, ginger, mustard, soy sauce, orange zest, and molasses.
2. Heat 2 tablespoon oil in the skillet and add salmon and cook for 5 to 7 minutes until fish becomes soft.
3. In a small frying pan, add oil. Heat and add vegetable mixture, salad dressings, and remaining ingredients.
4. Add salmon and stir gently.
5. Sprinkle sesame seeds and serve with rice.

Asian Glazed Chicken Thighs

Cooking Time: 25 minutes

Serving Size: 4

Calories: 274

Ingredients:

- 4 boneless skinless chicken thighs
- 3 garlic cloves, minced
- ¼ cup of rice vinegar
- ½ teaspoon ground ginger
- Toasted sesame seeds
- 2 teaspoons canola oil
- 3 tablespoons reduced-sodium soy sauce
- 2 tablespoons honey

Method:

1. Take a small bowl and blend honey, soy sauce, and vinegar.
2. In a large skillet, add 1 tablespoon of oil. Add chicken and heat until brown on each side.
3. Add blended mixture and heat for 2 minutes.
4. Add remaining ingredients and cook until it starts boiling.
5. Add in a dish and sprinkle sesame seeds. Serve with rice.

Mandarin Pork Stir-Fry

Cooking Time: 25 minutes

Serving Size: 4

Calories: 473

Ingredients:

- ½ teaspoon garlic powder
- 1 pork tenderloin (cut into 2-inch strips)

- ½ teaspoon ground ginger
- 2 tablespoons soy sauce
- 2 cups uncooked instant rice
- ½ cup of orange juice
- 1 package frozen sugar snap peas
- 1 can mandarin oranges, drained
- ¼ cup of water
- 1 tablespoon cornstarch
- 2 tablespoons canola oil

Method:
1. Follow package direction and cook rice according to these directions.
2. Take a bowl and mix garlic, ginger, and cornstarch.
3. Add orange juice and stir. Add soy sauce and water.
4. Mix until smooth and set aside.
5. Take a large skillet and add 1 tablespoon oil.
6. Add pork and stir fry until lightly brown. Set aside.
7. Add peas in the same skillet and boil until tender.
8. Add orange mixture and pork in skillet.
9. Stir fry for 2 minutes and remove. Serve with rice.

Hoisin-Pineapple Salmon

Cooking Time: 20 minutes

Serving Size: 4

Calories: 349

Ingredients:

- ¼ teaspoon pepper

- ½ cup unsweetened crushed pineapple
- 4 salmon fillets
- ¼ cup orange marmalade
- 2 tablespoons chopped fresh cilantro
- 2 tablespoons hoisin sauce

Method:
1. Heat oven at 400°F.
2. Prepare baking pan and grease with oil. Spread salmon and hoisin sauce.
3. Bake for 15 to 20 minutes or when fish begins to flake.
4. Take a small saucepan and mix pineapple with orange marmalade.
5. Bring to boil and stir continuously.
6. Pour over salmon and sprinkle coriander leaves.

Tropical Sweet and Spicy Pork Tenderloin

Cooking Time: 30 minutes

Serving Size: 4

Calories: 539

Ingredients:
- 2 finely chopped chipotle peppers
- 2 tablespoons olive oil
- 1 medium onion, chopped
- 1 medium green pepper, chopped
- 1 pork tenderloin cut into 1-inches cubes
- 3 garlic cloves, minced
- 1 cup chicken stock

- 1 can pineapple tidbits, drained
- ¼ teaspoon salt
- ¼ teaspoon pepper
- 2 tablespoons reduced-sodium soy sauce
- Hot cooked rice
- ½ cup packed brown sugar
- 1 cup honey barbecue sauce
- 2 teaspoons adobo sauce

Method:
1. Take a large skillet. Heat and add oil.
2. Sprinkle salt and pepper on pork and stir fry for 5 to 7 minutes.
3. Remove when cooked from both sides.
4. Take a pan and add ginger, garlic, chicken stock, onion.
5. Stir for 3 minutes.
6. Add remaining ingredients and cook for 5 minutes.
7. Add pork and cook until tender.
8. Remove and serve with rice.

5.2 Chinese Desserts Recipes

Chinese Almond Cookies

Cooking Time: 40 minutes

Serving Size: 30

Calories: 660

Ingredients:

- ½ teaspoon baking soda

- 2 cups flour
- ½ teaspoon baking powder
- ¼ teaspoon salt
- 2 ½ teaspoons almond extract
- 30 whole almonds
- ½ cup shortening
- ¾ cup white sugar
- 1 egg
- ½ cup butter
- 1 egg beaten

Method:
1. Heat Oven at 325°F.
2. Take a large bowl and add flour.
3. Add salt and mix well.
4. Add baking soda and baking powder. Stir well.
5. In a small bowl, beat butter, shortening, and sugar.
6. Add almond and egg in butter mixture and blend well.
7. Add flour mixture and blend until smooth.
8. Knead the dough and cut into 2 pieces.
9. Refrigerate for 2 hours.
10. Cut the dough into 14 to 15 pieces lengthwise.
11. Grease cookie tray and roll each piece in the round motion.
12. Put round balls into a cookie tray and add almonds in the center of each ball.
13. Grease cookies with beaten egg using a brush.

14. Bake for 15 to 20 minutes until golden brown.
15. Remove and let it cool. Serve when cold and crispy.

Nian Gao

Cooking Time: 60 minutes

Serving Size: 10

Calories: 338

Ingredients:

- 2 ½ cups milk
- One can red azuki beans
- 16 ounces mochiko sweet rice flour
- 1 to 1 ¾ cup sugar
- 1 tablespoon baking soda
- ½ cup unsalted butter
- ¾ cup of vegetable oil
- 3 eggs

Method:

1. Heat oven at 350°F.
2. Grease pan with butter or oil using spray or brush.
3. Mix all ingredients except beans in a processor and blend until smooth.
4. Sprinkle mochiko flour on the baking dish and add half batter.
5. Spread beans on top and add another layer of remaining batter on beans.
6. Bake for 40 to 45 minutes until cooked.
7. Check by using a toothpick if baked well.

8. Serve cold.

Eight Treasure Rice Pudding

Cooking Time: 105 minutes

Serving Size: 8

Calories: 432

Ingredients:

For the Rice:

- 1 cup black raisins
- 1 cup yellow raisins
- ¼ teaspoon salt

For the Fruit:

- Neutral oil for coating bowl
- 2 cups glutinous rice
- 1 tablespoon sunflower oil
- 1 cup sugar-glazed cherries
- 1 dried apricot

For the Filling:

- 1 cup sugar lotus seeds
- 100 grams red bean paste

For the Starch Water:

- 3 tablespoons water
- 2 teaspoon potato starch

For the Sugar Syrup:

- 1 tablespoon honey
- 1 tablespoon sugar

- ½ cup of water

Method:
1. Take a large bowl and put rice in it.
2. Add cold water and cover for 1 hour.
3. Drain and soak rice and steam for 40 minutes in simmering water.
4. Add oil and salt. Combine gently to prevent breaking rice.
5. Cut fruits in small pieces.
6. Take a bowl and grease with oil.
7. Add fruits and a layer of rice. Press gently.
8. Add red bean paste on it and spread with a spoon.
9. Place rice and cherries layer again.
10. Place the bowl in simmering water and steam for 30 minutes.
11. Take a small bowl and mix potato starch water ingredients.
12. Stir until well combined.
13. Place all syrup ingredients and bring to boil. Add starch water and boil for 10 minutes.
14. Remove the bowl from the water and invert it into the dish. Add sugary syrup on top.

Chinese Almond Float Dessert

Cooking Time: 60 minutes

Serving Size: 6

Calories: 312

Ingredients:

- 1 cup of cold water
- 1 can fruit cocktail with syrup
- 1 envelope unflavored gelatin
- 2 teaspoons almond extract
- 1 cup evaporated milk
- 4 tablespoons granulated sugar
- 1 cup boiling water

Method:

1. Take a small bowl and mix sugar with gelatin. Mix well.
2. Add boiling water in the gelatin mixture and stir continuously until dissolved.
3. Add almond extract, milk, and cold water. Mix well.
4. Wait until cool down. Cut into pieces and serve with can fruit.

Candied Banana Fritters

Cooking Time: 30 minutes

Serving Size: 4

Calories: 634

Ingredients:

- 3 to 6 tablespoons white sesame seeds
- ¾ cup of water
- 4 cups oil for deep-frying
- 1 egg, lightly beaten
- 1 cup all-purpose flour

- 5 bananas, firm
- 1 ½ cups granulated sugar
- 2 tablespoons oil

Method:

1. Cut bananas in small pieces about 1 ½ inch.
2. Combine water, egg, and flour. Stir and make the batter.
3. Heat oil in the frying pan. Take a banana slice and dip into the batter.
4. Carefully dip all slices and add them into hot oil for deep frying.
5. Fry until looks golden brown and batter is crispy.
6. Take a bowl and add cold water with ice cubes. Put it into the freezer.
7. Heat oil and add sugar. Stir until golden brown. Avoid high flame. It can cause sugar to burn.
8. Remove the wok and put it into cold water.
9. Use a stick to coat banana slices in syrup and add immediately into cold water until syrup is hardened.
10. Place in a dish and repeat with all slices.

Chinese Bow Tie Dessert with Honey and Brown Sugar

Cooking Time: 35 minutes

Serving Size: 16

Calories: 119

Ingredients:

- 4 to 6 cups oil
- 1 package egg roll wrappers

For the Syrup:
- ½ cup honey
- 1 cup brown sugar
- ½ cup of corn syrup
- ½ cup of water

Method:
1. Cut egg roll wrappers into four equal pieces.
2. Use 2 knives and make a knot like a bow tie on wrappers.
3. Heat wok and then add oil.
4. Fry bow tie for 5 minutes.
5. Boil syrup ingredients for 5 minutes.
6. Dip bow tie in sugar syrup and set aside.

Five-Spice Peanuts

Cooking Time: 40 minutes

Serving Size: 8

Calories: 266

Ingredients:
- 1 tablespoon light corn syrup
- 2 tablespoons butter
- ¼ cup brown sugar
- ½ teaspoon five-spice powder
- 2 cups unsalted peanuts

Method:
1. Take a baking tray and grease with oil.
2. In a large pan, melt butter, syrup, and sugar.

3. Heat on low flame and add five spices powder. Stir well.
4. Boil for 5 minutes and do not stir when it starts boiling.
5. Add on the baking sheet and mix peanuts. Wait to cool down and harden.
6. Cut into pieces and serve cold.

Chinese Sponge Cake

Cooking Time: 40 minutes

Serving Size: 3

Calories: 468

Ingredients:

- ½ tsp. cream of tartar
- ¾ cup sugar
- 1 cupcake flour
- 5 eggs
- 1 tsp. Baking powder
- ¼ tsp. salt
- 1 tsp. almond extract

Method:

1. Prepare pan and wok for steam.
2. Take a large bowl and mix flour, salt, baking powder, and baking soda. Stir well.
3. Take a bowl and separate egg whites from egg yolks. Beat egg whites until fluffy. Add cream and beat.
4. Add ¼ cup of sugar and beat again for 1 minute.
5. Add egg yolk in remaining sugar. Beat for 2 minutes and add almond extract.

6. Gradually add the egg mixture into the flour mixture.
7. Mix with a rubber spatula and set aside.
8. Pour batter into pan and heat wok.
9. Add water in the wok. Wait until it starts boiling.
10. Turn flame to medium and steam cake for 20 to 25 minutes covered.
11. Invert in the plate and cut into pieces.

Dairy-Free Mango Pudding

Cooking Time: 20 minutes

Serving Size: 4

Calories: 259

Ingredients:
- ¼ cup white sugar
- 1 cup good-quality coconut milk
- 1 packet gelatin
- 2 medium to large ripe mangoes
- ½ cup hot water

Method:
1. Take ripe mangoes and peel.
2. Blend mangoes in a processor until smooth. Set aside.
3. Take a pan and add water. Bring to boil.
4. Gradually add gelatin in water. Add milk and sugar.
5. Stir and blend with mango mixture.
6. Pour in a bowl and refrigerate for 2 hours.

Delicious Chinese Raspberry Snowflake Cake

Cooking Time: 25 minutes

Serving Size: 1 cake

Calories: 330

Ingredients:

Raspberry Snowflake Cake

- 450 milliliters water
- 125 grams of potato starch or corn flour
- 3 tablespoons desiccated coconut
- 55 grams raspberries
- 60 milliliters double cream
- 5 leaves gelatin
- 200 grams of sugar
- 200 milliliters whole milk

Coconut Milk Snowflake Cake

- 5 leaves gelatin
- 250 milliliters coconut milk
- 60 milliliters double cream
- 3 tablespoons desiccated coconut
- 125 grams of potato starch or corn flour
- 450 milliliters water
- 200 grams caster sugar

Method:

1. Take a small saucepan and cook water, raspberry, and sugar.

2. Keep whisking until boil and raspberry completely dissolve in sugar.
3. Let it cool down.
4. Add double cream and milk into raspberry jam and bring to boil.
5. Rest aside for 10 minutes and add gelatin. Stir well.
6. Add starch and 100ml additional water.
7. Prepare a baking tray and put mixture.
8. Keep in the refrigerator for 3 hours.
9. Slice and sprinkle coconut. Serve cold.

Fortune Cookies

Cooking Time: 30 minutes

Serving Size: 10

Calories: 133

Ingredients:
- 3 tablespoons vegetable oil
- 8 tablespoons sugar
- ½ teaspoon almond extract
- 3 teaspoons water
- 8 tablespoons all-purpose flour
- 2 large egg whites
- ½ teaspoon vanilla extract
- 1 ½ teaspoons cornstarch
- ¼ teaspoon salt

Method:
1. Heat oven at 300°F.
2. Beat egg, vanilla and almond extract, and vegetable oil in a bowl.
3. Take a large bowl and mix starch, flour, and water. Blend until smooth.
4. Add egg mixture into the flour mixture and blend to make the batter.
5. Grease baking pan with sheet and oil. Add batter with a spoon on sheet.
6. Put that paper in the middle of the cookies and fold edges.
7. Bake for 14 to 16 minutes until brown and crispy.

Chapter 6: Chinese Traditional Wok Recipes and Vegetarian Chinese Meals

6.1 Chinese Famous Wok Recipes

Spicy Oyster Sauce Squid with Green Peppers

Cooking Time: 15 minutes

Serving Size: 2

Calories: 512

Ingredients:

- 1 tablespoon low-sodium light soy sauce
- 1 green pepper (sliced into cubes)
- ½ teaspoon dark soy sauce
- 1 teaspoon oyster sauce
- 1 tablespoon rapeseed oil
- 1 medium white onion (cut into slices)

- 1 tablespoon fresh lemon juice
- A pinch of caster sugar
- 1 red chili (finely chopped)
- 200g whole baby squid (sliced into rings)
- 1 tablespoon rice vinegar

Method:
1. Heat wok and add 1 tablespoon oil.
2. Add sliced onion and rapeseed oil. Heat for 20 minutes until brown and crispy.
3. Add squid and red chili. Heat for 10 seconds. Add rice vinegar.
4. Add green pepper and stir for 1 minute.
5. Add 1 tablespoon water around the edges of the wok to create steam.
6. Cook for 1 minute more and add remaining ingredients.
7. Stir and serve immediately.

Vegetarian Hokkien Mee

Cooking Time: 22 minutes

Serving Size: 2

Calories: 522

Ingredients:
- A knob of fresh ginger (grated)
- 100g Quorn mince
- 1 tablespoon low-sodium light soy sauce
- A drizzle of toasted sesame oil

- 1 tablespoon rapeseed oil
- 2 garlic cloves (chopped)
- 1 teaspoon dark soy sauce
- 2 mini sweet shallots (chopped)
- 1 red chili (chopped)
- 400g cooked egg noodles (200g dried)
- 100g fresh beansprouts
- 3 dried Chinese mushrooms (soaked and finely diced)
- 100ml hot vegetable stock

For Garnish

- Spring onions (sliced)
- Red chili, (sliced into rings)

Method:

1. Heat wok on high flame. Add the rapeseed oil and stir.
2. Add garlic, ginger, chili, and shallots.
3. Heat and stir to explode flavors in the wok for 1 minute.
4. Add dark soy sauce, mushroom, and Quorn. Leave for 2 minutes.
5. Add soy sauce and vegetable stock. Cook for 10 minutes.
6. Add cooked egg noodles and spread sesame oil over it.
7. Stir and serve.
8. You can serve noodles separately in two bowls with the mixture on top of the noodles.

Beijing Egg and Tomato Noodle Soup

Cooking Time: 15 minutes

Serving Size: 2

Calories: 479

Ingredients:

- 1 tablespoon vegetable bouillon powder
- 300g cooked rice noodles (150g uncooked)
- 250g tomatoes (cored and quartered)
- 100g Chinese cabbage (cut into slices)
- 1 tablespoon sesame oil
- 1 tablespoon light soy sauce
- A pinch of white pepper
- 1 egg (beaten)
- 2 spring onions (sliced, to garnish)
- 1 root ginger (peeled and grated)
- 5 fresh shiitake mushrooms (dried and cut into slices)

Method:

1. Heat wok and add ginger, garlic, mushrooms, vegetable powder, and tomatoes.
2. Add 1-liter water in the wok and bring to boil.
3. Cook for 2 minutes until vegetables get softened.
4. Reduce heat to medium and add rice noodles. Add soy sauce and sesame oil.
5. Add remaining ingredients and stir.
6. Add beaten eggs and stir continuously for 2 minutes.
7. Immediately remove from heat and serve.

Radish in Black Rice Vinegar with Crabmeat and Black Sesame Seeds

Cooking Time: 10 minutes

Serving Size: 2

Calories: 333

Ingredients:

- 1 teaspoon rapeseed oil
- 5g black sesame seed (garnish)
- Dried chili flakes (garnish)
- 200g radishes (cut into slices)
- 1 tablespoon black rice vinegar
- 300g radish leaves
- A pinch of caster sugar
- 200g fresh white crab meat

Method:

1. Heat wok on high flame and add the rapeseed oil. Wait for 30 seconds.
2. Add radish sliced and radish leaves in the wok.
3. Stir and add water on the edges of the wok to make steam.
4. Cook for 10 seconds and add remaining ingredients.
5. Remove from heat and serve in a separate dish.
6. Garnish chili flakes and sesame seed on top of the radish.

Lobster Tails, Baby Asparagus and Eggs in Hot Bean Sauce

Cooking Time: 15 minutes

Serving Size: 2

Calories: 230

Ingredients:
- 1 teaspoon corn flour
- 2 spring onions
- 100ml hot vegetable stock
- 1 egg (beaten)
- 1 tablespoon rapeseed oil
- 2 garlic cloves (chopped)
- 200g cooked fresh lobster (sliced into cubes)
- 100g baby asparagus spears
- 1 teaspoon yellow bean paste
- ½ teaspoon dark soy sauce
- 1 tablespoon light soy sauce
- 1 ginger (peeled and grated)
- 1 red chili (chopped)

Method:
1. Heat wok on high flame and add the rapeseed oil. Toss for 5 minutes.
2. Add ginger, garlic, and chili and stir for 2 minutes to release flavor.
3. Add lobsters and stir for 1 minute. Add asparagus and toss for 1 minute more.
4. Add 1 tablespoon water on the edges of the wok to give steam.
5. Add light and dark soy sauce. Stir and add yellow bean paste.
6. Add egg and bring it to boil.

7. Mix the corn flour into 2 tablespoon water and add it into the wok.
8. Stir continuously until thickens.
9. Garnish with onions and serve immediately.

Pineapple Chicken

Cooking Time: 12 minutes

Serving Size: 2

Calories: 240.4

Ingredients:
- A pinch of black pepper
- 1 tablespoon corn flour
- ½ small pineapple (cubes)
- fresh coriander leaves (to garnish)
- 1 tablespoon rapeseed oil
- ½ red pepper (cubes)
- 250g boneless chicken thighs (sliced into cubes)
- sea salt flakes
- 1 spring onion (sliced)
- 2 dried chilies
- roasted cashew nuts

For the Sauce
- 1 teaspoon honey
- ¼ teaspoon Sriracha chili sauce
- 1 tablespoon corn flour
- 100ml pineapple juice

- 1 tablespoon light soy sauce
- 1 lime juice

Method:

1. Take a large bowl and add chicken. Sprinkle pepper and salt. Add corn flour and mix to combine. Set aside.
2. Take all ingredients of the sauce and mix it in a blender. Set aside.
3. Heat a wok on high flame and add the rapeseed oil.
4. Add red chili and stir for flavor.
5. Add chicken pieces and toss for 5 minutes.
6. Add red pepper and pineapple. Cook for 30 seconds.
7. Add sauce and cook until sticky.
8. Add remaining ingredients and cook for 2 minutes more.
9. Remove from flame and garnish with coriander leaves.

Buddha's Stir-Fried Mixed Vegetables

Cooking Time: 15 minutes

Serving Size: 2

Calories: 500

Ingredients:

- 1 tablespoon rapeseed oil
- Ginger root (peeled and grated)
- 4 fresh shiitake mushrooms (dried and sliced)
- 1 cup dried wood ear mushrooms
- 1 cup of fresh beansprouts
- 1 medium carrot

- 1 cup of baby sweetcorn
- ½ teaspoon salted black beans (crushed with rice vinegar 1 tablespoon)
- 1 can of bamboo shoots
- 2 spring onions (garnish)

For the sauce

- 1 tablespoon light soy sauce
- 1 tablespoon vegetarian mushroom sauce
- 100 ml cold vegetable stock
- 1 teaspoon toasted sesame oil
- 1 tablespoon corn flour

Method:

1. Mix all ingredients of sauce in a blender and blend until smooth. Set aside.
2. Heat a wok on high flame and add the rapeseed oil.
3. Add ginger and fry on low heat. Add beans paste and cook for 1 minute.
4. Add vegetables and remaining ingredients except for beansprout. Whisk well.
5. Add sauce and cook for 5 minutes until sticky.
6. Add beansprout and heat for 30 seconds.
7. Transfer to a dish and garnish with onion.

Penang Curry with Chicken

Cooking Time: 35 minutes

Serving Size: 4

Calories: 596

Ingredients:

- 2 peppers fresh red chili peppers
- ¼ cup fresh basil leaves
- 2 tablespoons palm sugar
- 4 cups of coconut milk
- ⅔ pound skinless (boneless and cubed)
- 2 tablespoons fish sauce
- 5 tablespoons Penang curry paste
- cooking oil
- 6 leaf kaffir lime leaves

Method:

1. Heat wok on high flame and add the rapeseed oil.
2. Add curry paste and stir for 2 minutes.
3. Add coconut milk and wait until boiling.
4. Add chicken pieces and cook for 15 minutes.
5. Add remaining ingredients and stir for 2 minutes.
6. Garnish with basil leaves.

Thai Spicy Basil Chicken Fried Rice

Cooking Time: 40 minutes

Serving Size: 6

Calories: 794.1

Ingredients:

- 1 teaspoon white sugar
- ½ cup cilantro sprigs
- 2 peppers serrano peppers (crushed)

- 1 onion (sliced)
- 2 cups sweet basil
- 1-pound boneless chicken breast
- ½ cup sesame oil for frying
- 5 cups jasmine rice (cooked)
- 6 garlic clove (crushed)
- 1 cucumber (sliced)
- 3 tablespoons oyster sauce
- 2 tablespoons fish sauce
- 2 red pepper (sliced)

Method:
1. Take a bowl and mix fish sauce, sugar, and oyster sauce.
2. Heat wok on high flame and add the rapeseed oil.
3. Add serrano pepper and garlic. Stir for 1 minute.
4. Add chicken and sauce mixture. Cook for 5 minutes.
5. Add remaining ingredients except for rice and cook for 10 minutes.
6. Add rice and stir continuously to prevent sticking.
7. Remove from flame and garnish with coriander leaves.

Chinese Buffet Green Beans

Cooking Time: 25 minutes

Serving Size: 6

Calories: 54.5

Ingredients:

- 1-pound fresh green beans (trimmed)
- 2 tablespoons oyster sauce
- 2 teaspoons soy sauce
- 1 tablespoon oil sesame
- 2 cloves garlic (sliced)
- 1 tablespoon white sugar

Method:

1. Heat wok on high flame and add sesame oil.
2. Add garlic and white sugar. Heat until brown.
3. Add green beans and remaining ingredients.
4. Bring to boil and cook for 15 minutes until beans are softened.
5. Garnish with sesame seed and serve.

Summer Special Shrimp and Fruit Fried Rice

Cooking Time: 60 minutes

Serving Size: 2

Calories: 590.8

Ingredients:

- 6 halves walnuts
- 2 cups cold, cooked white rice
- 2 large eggs (beaten)
- 1 tablespoon vegetable oil
- 1 piece of ginger root
- 1 tablespoon soy sauce
- 2 tablespoons cilantro

- ⅔ cup fresh pineapple
- 2 red onions
- 3 green chili peppers
- ½ cup orange segments
- ½ pound shrimp
- salt and pepper

Method:
1. Heat wok on medium flame and add 1 tablespoon oil.
2. Add onion and stir until brown. Set aside.
3. Heat wok on high flame and add shrimp.
4. Stir continuously for 10 minutes until no longer pink in color. Set aside.
5. Wipe wok and heat on high flame. Add ginger, onion, and garlic in 1 tablespoon oil.
6. Stir and heat for 3 minutes until brown on edges.
7. Add pineapple and orange. Stir until pineapple becomes hot.
8. Add remaining ingredients and stir. Add shrimp and onion. Stir for 3 minutes.
9. Garnish with cilantro and serve.

6.2 World Renowned Chinese Recipes

Sichuan Hot Pot

Cooking Time: 1 hour 10 minutes

Serving Size: 1 hot pot

Calories: 259

Ingredients:

For Soup Base:
- 12-14 cups chicken stock
- 10 cloves garlic
- 1 cinnamon stick
- 2 tablespoons oil
- 10 cloves
- 1 tablespoon Sichuan peppercorns
- 10 whole red chilies
- 6 slices ginger
- 3-4 bay leaves
- 1 package spicy hot pot soup base
- 5-star anise

For Dipping Sauce
- Sesame seeds
- Peanuts
- Sesame paste
- Sesame oil
- Cilantro
- Soy sauce
- Chinese black vinegar
- Scallions
- Sacha sauce
- Chili oil
- Garlic

Hot Pot Sides:

- Thinly shaved beef
- Sliced chicken
- Prepared frozen dumplings
- Chinese rice cakes
- Fresh noodles
- Bok choy
- Assorted fish balls
- Thinly sliced fish fillets
- Napa cabbage
- Shiitake mushrooms
- Tofu sheets
- Glass noodles
- Firm tofu
- Soy puffs
- Straw mushrooms
- Green leaf lettuce
- Wood ear mushrooms

Method:

1. To make soup, heat wok and add 1 tablespoon oil and ginger.
2. Stir for 2 minutes. Add garlic, bay leaves, cinnamon stick, cloves, and star anise.
3. Cook for 5 minutes for flavors.
4. Add hot pot soup base, chilies, and peppercorn. Cook for another 2 minutes.

5. Add chicken stock and wait until it starts boiling. Transfer to a broad and deep pot. Set aside
6. Mix all ingredients of dipping sauce and blend until smooth. Set aside.
7. Prepare a hot plate and plugin. Add broth and bring to boil.
8. Pour hot pot side ingredients that you like to add and cook until boil.
9. Place dipping sauce and soup. Serve in the pot.

Braised Pork Ball in Gravy

Cooking Time: 15 minutes

Serving Size: 4

Calories: 684.6

Ingredients:

For meatballs:

- 1 teaspoon salt
- 1 tablespoon dark soy sauce
- 100-gram corn starch
- 1000-gram pork
- 1 leftover steamed bun
- scallion 20 grams
- 2 tablespoon light soy sauce
- 2 tablespoon Shaoxing wine
- 1 cup oil
- 2-gram ginger

For Sauce:

- Sugar ¼ tablespoon
- Corn starch 1 tablespoon
- Dark soy sauce ¼ tablespoon
- 2 slices fresh ginger
- Light soy sauce ½ tablespoon
- Water 1 cup

Method:

1. Add meatball ingredients in a pan and stir continuously in one direction for 5 minutes.
2. Make small round meatballs and set aside.
3. Take all ingredients of the sauce and mix it in a wok or pan.
4. Add oil and stir for 10 minutes.
5. Add meatballs and cook for 30 seconds.
6. Serve hot with rice.

Steamed Garlic Prawns with Vermicelli

Cooking Time: 17 minutes

Serving Size: 2

Calories: 143

Ingredients:

- 10 tiger prawns
- 2 tablespoon light soy sauce
- ¼ teaspoon sugar
- 1 tablespoon cooking oil
- 100 g mung bean vermicelli noodles

- 1 tablespoon water
- 2 tablespoon minced garlic
- 2 tablespoon chopped fresh chili
- 1 tablespoon Shaoxing rice wine
- ¼ teaspoon white pepper
- 1 pinch salt
- scallions for garnishing

Method:
1. Soak noodles and add 1 tablespoon oil to avoid sticking. Set aside.
2. Cut and peel prawns. Put them on noodles.
3. Heat the pan and add oil. Add garlic, water, chili, white pepper, rice wine, soy sauce, and sugar. Heat for 5 minutes until flavored.
4. Add sauce over prawns and noodles.
5. Steam for 5 minutes and serve hot.

Peking Duck

Cooking Time: 1 hour 35 minutes

Serving Size: 4

Calories: 555.7

Ingredients:
- ¼ teaspoon white pepper
- ⅛ teaspoon cloves
- ½ cup plum jam
- 3 tablespoons soy sauce
- 1 tablespoon honey

- 5 green onions
- 1 orange
- 1 tablespoon parsley
- 1 whole duck
- ½ teaspoon cinnamon
- ½ teaspoon ginger
- ¼ teaspoon nutmeg
- 1 ½ teaspoons sugar
- 1 ½ teaspoon white vinegar

Method:
1. Wash duck from inner side and outer side.
2. Mix cinnamon, white pepper, ginger, nutmeg, and cloves.
3. Sprinkle spices mixture on the duck.
4. Add 1 tablespoon vinegar and pour it on the duck.
5. Spread with hands and refrigerate for at least 2 hours.
6. Take a wok and add water. Steam duck from the breast side for 1 hour.
7. Pour lime juice and green onions.
8. Heat oven at 375°F.
9. Remove the skin of the duck and put it in the pan to roast.
10. Roast for 30 minutes. Mix honey with 3 tablespoon soy sauce.
11. Brush it on duck and roast for more than 10 minutes.
12. Mix sugar, chutney, and vinegar to make the sauce.

13. Garnish with parsley and orange slices.

Shrimp Rice Noodle Rolls

Cooking Time: 15 minutes

Serving Size: 8

Calories: 118

Ingredients:

For Shrimp:

- ½ teaspoon sugar
- ¼ teaspoon baking soda
- 2 tablespoons water
- ½ teaspoon cornstarch
- ¼ teaspoon sesame oil
- ¼ teaspoon salt
- 8 ounces shrimp
- ¼ teaspoon white pepper

For Sauce:

- 1 teaspoon oyster sauce
- 1 teaspoon oil
- 2 teaspoons dark soy sauce
- 5 teaspoons sugar
- 1 scallion
- 6 slices ginger
- 2 ½ tablespoons light soy sauce
- ¼ cup of water
- Salt

For the Rice Noodle Rolls:

- 1 cup of water
- Vegetable or canola oil
- 5 tablespoons rice flour
- 1 tablespoon mung bean starch
- 2 tablespoons wheat starch
- 2 tablespoons cornstarch
- ¼ teaspoon salt

Method:

1. Coat shrimps with baking soda, sugar, and water.
2. Refrigerate for 2 hours and wash thoroughly.
3. Coat shrimp with white pepper, sesame oil, cornstarch, and salt.
4. Cover and refrigerate for 1 hour.
5. Mix all ingredients of sauce and heat on low flame.
6. Cook until smooth.
7. Wet a clean cloth and set aside.
8. Steam shrimps for 10 minutes and put in a bowl.
9. Add rice noodles and add shrimps.
10. Cover with wet cloth and roll.
11. Remove the cloth and cut rice noodles lengthwise.
12. Serve with sauce.

Mapo Tofu

Cooking Time: 35 minutes

Serving Size: 6

Calories: 335

Ingredients:
- ¼ teaspoon sugar
- 6-8 dried red chilies
- 1 ½ tablespoon Sichuan peppercorns
- 3 tablespoons ginger
- 3 tablespoons garlic
- ¼ cup low sodium chicken broth
- 1-pound silken tofu
- 1 scallion
- ½ cup oil
- 1-2 fresh chili peppers
- 1 ½ teaspoons cornstarch
- ¼ teaspoon sesame oil
- 8 ounces pork
- 1-2 tablespoons spicy bean sauce

Method:
1. Heat wok and add chilies in oil. Stir for 5 minutes for the fragment. Set aside.
2. Heat wok and add oil. Add peppercorn, garlic, and ginger. Cook for 7 minutes.
3. Add ground pork and cook until pink color disappears.
4. Add bean mixture and chicken broth. Stir well.
5. Add water in cornstarch. Mix and add into bean mixture.
6. Add remaining ingredients and seasonings. Stir for 10 minutes.

7. Serve hot and garnish with onion.

Yang Chow Fried Rice

Cooking Time: 35 minutes

Serving Size: 6

Calories: 301

Ingredients:
- 2 teaspoons salt
- 10 pieces shrimps
- 1 teaspoon garlic
- 3 tablespoons cooking oil
- ¼ cup green onion
- 2 pieces of raw eggs beaten
- 1 teaspoon sugar
- 6 cups cooked white rice
- 1 cup barbecued pork
- 1 ½ tablespoons soy sauce
- ¾ cup green peas
- 1 teaspoon ginger

Method:
1. Take a pan and heat garlic and ginger in oil.
2. Add shrimps and cook for 5 minutes. Set aside.
3. Add eggs and stir for 30 seconds.
4. Add rice in egg and mix thoroughly.
5. Add sauce, sugar, and other spices.
6. Add barbecue pork and cook for 5 minutes.

7. Add shrimp and green peas. Cook for 5 minutes.
8. Add green onions and cook for 1 minute.
9. Transfer to plate and serve.

Wonton Soup

Cooking Time: 40 minutes

Serving Size: 6

Calories: 289.6

Ingredients:

- 2 bok choy
- 2 cloves garlic
- 1 tablespoon ginger
- 4 cups chicken broth
- 3 green onions
- 1 tablespoon sesame oil
- 4 ounces shiitake mushrooms
- 1 tablespoon yellow miso paste

For Wontons

- 1 tablespoon reduced-sodium soy sauce
- 1 tablespoon ginger
- 1 tablespoon oyster sauce
- 1 teaspoon sesame oil
- 8 ounces medium shrimp
- 2 cloves garlic
- 2 green onions
- ½ teaspoon Sriracha

- ¼ teaspoon black pepper
- 36 wonton wrappers

Method:
1. Take a large bowl and combine garlic, ginger, shrimp, Sriracha, soy sauce, sesame oil, and oyster sauce.
2. Put wonton wrappers and pour 1 tablespoon shrimp mixture over it.
3. Fold wrappers and press edges to seal.
4. Take a pan and heat on low flame.
5. Add garlic, ginger, and chicken broth.
6. Add 2 cups water and bring to boil.
7. Add mushrooms and cook for 10 minutes.
8. Add green onions, bok choy, miso paste, and cook for 3 minutes.
9. Add wonton and stir for 2 minutes.
10. Serve hot with sauce.

Chinese Egg Fried Rice

Cooking Time: 20 minutes

Serving Size: 2

Calories: 163

Ingredients:
- 1 big onion diced
- 3 eggs beaten
- 2 spring onion
- 3 tablespoon vegetable oil
- 3 cups cooked rice

Seasonings:
- 2 tablespoon light soy sauce
- 1 teaspoon salt
- ½ teaspoon ground white pepper

Method:
1. Beat eggs and cut vegetables.
2. Heat a wok on high flame and add 1 tablespoon oil.
3. Add eggs and stir continuously.
4. Remove eggs from heat and set aside.
5. Heat wok again and add 1 tablespoon oil.
6. Add eggs and stir immediately. Do not burn the rice.
7. Add vegetables and salt, pepper.
8. Mix again and add soy sauce from the edges of the wok.
9. Cook for 2 minutes and serve hot with parsley and onion garnishing.

French Onion Rice

Cooking Time: 1 hour 30 minutes

Serving Size: 8

Calories: 135

Ingredients:
- 2 cup basmati rice
- 3 cup low-sodium beef broth
- 1 tablespoon thyme leaves
- 1 teaspoon freshly ground black pepper
- ¼ white wine

- 6 cloves garlic, minced
- Lemon wedges
- 6 tablespoon butter
- 1 tablespoon olive oil
- 2 large onions
- 1 ¼ teaspoon kosher salt

Method:
1. Take a large pan and heat. Add butter and onion.
2. Add salt and cook for 30 minutes until caramelized. Set aside.
3. Take a pan and add 1 tablespoon oil.
4. Add rice, garlic thyme, and lemon, wine, and stir well.
5. Add caramelized mixture ¾ and seasoning in rice. Combine and cook for 3 minutes.
6. Add broth and wait to boil.
7. Reduce heat and cook for 15 minutes.
8. Transfer to bowl and add remaining caramelized mixture. Garnish with thyme.

6.3 Recipes of Vegetarian Chinese Meals

15-Minute Garlic Noodles

Cooking Time: 15 minutes

Serving Size: 3

Calories: 426

Ingredients:
- 4 green onions

- 4 tablespoons peanut oil
- 2 teaspoon ginger
- 1 bell pepper
- 4 cloves garlic
- 6 oz. Chow Mein noodles

Sauce:

- 1 tablespoon soy sauce
- ½ teaspoon sesame oil
- ¼ cup chicken broth
- 2 tablespoons Shaoxing wine
- 2 tablespoons oyster sauce

Method:

1. Take a bowl and mix all ingredients of sauce until smooth.
2. Cook noodles by following directions on the package. Rinse with water and add 1 tablespoon oil to prevent sticking.
3. Add oil in a wok or pan and add noodles.
4. Stir noodles to prevent sticking to the wok.
5. Add vegetables and stir for 3 minutes.
6. Add sauce and mix well.
7. Cook for 1 minute and serve immediately.

General Tso Tofu

Cooking Time: 30 minutes

Serving Size: 3

Calories: 345

Ingredients:
- 1 tablespoon maple syrup
- 6 tablespoons cornstarch
- 1 block tofu
- 2 tablespoons soy sauce

Sauce:
- 2 teaspoons cornstarch
- 2 tablespoons Shaoxing wine
- ¼ cup chicken stock
- 2 tablespoons Chinkiang vinegar
- ¼ cup of sugar
- 1 tablespoon light soy sauce
- 1 tablespoon dark soy sauce

Stir fry:
- 2 teaspoons ginger
- 3 to 4 cloves garlic
- 3 tablespoons peanut oil
- 4 green onions
- 2 fresh Thai chili pepper
- 2 bunches broccoli

Method:
1. Marinate tofu with maple syrup and soy sauce in a sealing bag for 10 to 15 minutes.
2. Mix all ingredients of the sauce and stir until combine properly.

3. Gently open the bag of tofu and discard extra liquid. Add cornstarch and mix tofu well.
4. Heat wok and add 1 tablespoon oil.
5. Add broccoli and 3 tablespoon water. Cover immediately to cook broccoli in steam. Heat for 4 minutes and set aside.
6. Clean wok and add 1 tablespoon oil.
7. Add tofu in the wok and cook for 10 minutes until brown. Set aside.
8. Add remaining ingredients in wok and stir well until sauce becomes thick.
9. Transfer tofu on the plate. Pour broccoli and sauce. Serve with rice.

Nepali Momus with Spinach and Ricotta

Cooking Time: 50 minutes

Serving Size: 20

Calories: 75

Ingredients:
- ¼ cup parmesan cheese
- 2 green onions
- 20 round dumplings wrappers
- ¾ cup ricotta cheese
- 5 cups spinach leaves
- 1 clove garlic
- Freshly ground black pepper
- 1 tablespoon butter
- ¾ teaspoon salt

Method:
1. Take a skillet and add spinach and garlic. Add 3 tablespoon water and cook for 5 minutes until spinach wilted. Set aside.
2. Mix all ingredients except dumpling wraps.
3. Add 1 tablespoon mixture in each dumpling and wrap like half-moon shape.
4. Steam dumplings for 10 minutes until cook. Serve with sauce.

Real Deal Sesame Noodles

Cooking Time: 20 minutes

Serving Size: 4

Calories: 166

Ingredients:
- 2 green onions
- 250 grams of noodles

Peanut sauce:
- 2 cloves garlic
- ¼ teaspoon Sichuan peppercorn powder
- 2 tablespoons light soy sauce
- 2 tablespoons Chinkiang vinegar
- 1 tablespoon honey
- ¼ cup natural peanut butter
- 2 teaspoons chili oil
- 1 teaspoon sesame oil
- 1 teaspoon ginger

Topping options:

- tomatoes
- sesame seeds
- 1 cucumber
- 2 carrots

Method:

1. Cook noodles by following package directions. Rinse and add 1 tablespoon oil to prevent sticking.
2. Add peanut butter in warm water and make a smooth paste.
3. Add remaining ingredients and cook for 5 minutes until thick sauce forms.
4. Add noodles in a pan and add the sauce. Mix well. Garnish with sesame seeds and cucumber.

Homemade Vegetarian Oyster Sauce

Cooking Time: 20 minutes

Serving Size: 1

Calories: 40

Ingredients:

- 1 tablespoon dark soy sauce
- 1 teaspoon ginger
- 1 tablespoon light soy sauce
- 1 teaspoon agave syrup
- 2 teaspoons miso paste
- 1.4 oz. shiitake mushrooms
- 2 tablespoons peanut oil

- ¼ teaspoon five-spice powder
- 2 teaspoons sesame oil
- 2 cloves garlic

Method:

1. Wash shiitake mushroom and add hot water in it. Wait for 30 minutes until mushroom tender.
2. Dry mushrooms and cut into small pieces.
3. Take a wok and fry mushrooms in 1 tablespoon oil. Cook for 5 minutes.
4. Add ginger garlic and cook for 1 minute.
5. Add 1 cup of water in the blender and blend the mushroom mixture.
6. Transfer to the frying pan and add remaining ingredients. Add seasonings to taste and cook for 10 minutes.
7. Cooldown and store in a container for 1 week or refrigerator for 1 month.

Carrot Dumplings

Cooking Time: 20

Serving Size: 45 minutes

Calories: 38

Ingredients:

- 45 dumpling wrappers
- 2 teaspoons potato starch

Filling:
- 4 cloves garlic
- 1 tablespoon light soy sauce
- ½ teaspoon salt
- 1-pound carrots
- 3 large eggs
- 1 cup bamboo shoots
- 1 cup shiitake mushrooms
- 2 slices ginger
- 3 tablespoons sesame oil
- ¼ teaspoon white pepper powder

Sauce:
- 2 teaspoons light soy sauce
- 2 tablespoons black vinegar
- 2 teaspoons chili oil

Method:
1. Wash shiitake mushroom and add hot water in it. Wait for 30 minutes until mushroom tender.
2. Dry mushrooms and cut into small pieces.
3. Take a wok and fry mushrooms in 1 tablespoon oil. Cook for 5 minutes.
4. Add ginger, garlic, and carrot and cook for 1 minute.
5. Add 1 cup of water in the blender and blend the mushroom mixture.
6. Transfer to pan and cook until carrots soften. Add eggs and cook for 2 minutes.

7. Add soy sauce, bamboo shoots, salt, and white pepper. Mix and set aside.
8. Combine potato starch with water and brush on dumpling wraps.
9. Add 1 tablespoon mixture overwraps and seal dumplings.
10. Mix all ingredients of the sauce and stir until combine.
11. Steam dumplings for 8 to 10 minutes and serve with sauce.

Di San Xian

Cooking Time: 30 minutes

Serving Size: 2

Calories: 220

Ingredients:

- ½ tablespoon dark soy sauce
- 1 tablespoon Shaoxing wine
- ¼ cup vegetable stock
- ½ tablespoon sugar
- ¼ teaspoon salt
- 1 teaspoon cornstarch
- 1 tablespoon light soy sauce

Stir fry:

- 1 bell pepper
- 2 teaspoons sesame seeds for garnish
- ½ regular eggplant
- 2 green onion

- 2 cloves of garlic
- 2 teaspoons cornstarch
- ¼ cup peanut oil
- 1 small russet potato

Method:
1. Soak eggplants in water for 15 to 20 minutes and sprinkle salt over it.
2. Cut eggplant in small pieces and sprinkle cornstarch.
3. Mix cornstarch, salt, soy sauce, oil, and wine. Set aside.
4. Heat a skillet and add oil. Cook eggplants until golden brown.
5. Remove eggplant and add potato pieces in the skillet.
6. Add garlic and onion and stir fry.
7. Mix sauce until thicken.
8. Add remaining ingredients and eggplants. Mix and serve immediately.

Chinese Broccoli

Cooking Time: 20 minutes

Serving Size: 4

Calories: 90

Ingredients:
- 4 cloves garlic
- 1 bunch Chinese broccoli
- Pinch of salt
- ½ lb. white mushrooms
- 1 tablespoon peanut oil

Sauce:

- 1 tablespoon cornstarch
- 2 tablespoons soy sauce
- 1 cup vegetable stock
- 2 teaspoons sugar
- 1 teaspoon dark soy sauce

Method:

1. Mix all sauce ingredients and set aside.
2. Take a wok and add water. Add broccoli and steam for 5 minutes.
3. Remove excess water and add oil and garlic.
4. Cook for 3 minutes. Add mushroom until golden brown.
5. Add remaining ingredients and sauce. Cook for 2 minutes and serve.

Chinese Banana Fritters

Cooking Time: 25 minutes

Serving Size: 6

Calories: 196

Ingredients:

- Oil for deep frying
- Powdered sugar
- 5 big ripe bananas

Batter

- 1 tablespoon granulated sugar
- ½ cup cornstarch

- 2 tablespoons milk
- ½ cup all-purpose flour
- 1 tablespoon butter
- ½ cup of water

Method:
1. Combine all ingredients of batter and mix until smooth.
2. Heat oil in the pan. Add banana slices in batter and pour in hot oil.
3. Cook for 5 minutes until golden brown.
4. Serve with sugar or maple syrup.

Mango Sago

Cooking Time: 30 minutes

Serving Size: 4

Calories: 340

Ingredients:
- 1 cup full-fat coconut milk
- 2 big mangoes
- ¾ cup evaporated milk
- ½ grapefruit
- ¼ cup tapioca pearls
- ¼ cup of sugar

Method:
1. Boil water and add tapioca pearls until transparent. Add in sieve and merge with tapioca pearls. Set aside
2. Blend half mangoes in milk to make a smooth mixture. Add sugar and blend again.

3. Take a bowl and add tapioca pearls. Add mango paste and coconut oil. Garnish with mango slices.

Conclusion

Chinese foods are very different from all other foods in different countries. Ingredients and taste can vary from region to region in China too, but their preparation method is almost identical. Chinese foods have been prevailing since ancient times and are widely famous for their unique taste and healthy ingredients. There are many benefits of eating Chinese food as it provides nutrients that a body needs and it also uses fewer fat ingredients. Rice is the leading food item in China that is served with every dish and in every meal. Buddhists who cannot consume meat can eat vegetarian dishes. The basic techniques of Chinese food are frying, deep-frying, steaming, boiling, and roasting. Chinese food made at home is very different from the food available at restaurants. There are many health benefits to consuming Chinese food. It helps to regulate your body fluids and enhance your metabolism. Thus, Chinese food is famous in America for its flavors and cooking styles. Vegetarians, lacto-Ovo-vegetarians, Buddhists, Ovo-vegetarians, etc., all can eat Chinese foods due to a wide variety of cooking techniques.

Japanese Home Cooking

Learn How to Prepare Japanese Traditional Food with Over 100 Recipes for Ramen, Sushi, and Vegetarian Dishes

By

Adele Tyler

© **Copyright 2020 by Adele Tyler - All rights reserved.**

This document is geared towards providing exact and reliable information in regard to the topic and issue covered. The publication is sold with the idea that the publisher is not required to render accounting, officially permitted, or otherwise, qualified services. If advice is necessary, legal or professional, a practiced individual in the profession should be ordered.

From a Declaration of Principles which was accepted and approved equally by a Committee of the American Bar Association and a Committee of Publishers and Associations.

In no way is it legal to reproduce, duplicate, or transmit any part of this document in either electronic means or in printed format. Recording of this publication is strictly prohibited and any storage of this document is not allowed unless with written permission from the publisher. All rights reserved.

The information provided herein is stated to be truthful and consistent, in that any liability, in terms of inattention or otherwise, by any usage or abuse of any policies, processes, or directions contained within is the solitary and utter responsibility of the recipient reader. Under no circumstances will any legal responsibility or blame be held against the publisher for any reparation, damages, or monetary loss due to the information herein, either directly or indirectly.

Respective authors own all copyrights not held by the publisher.

The information herein is offered for informational purposes solely and is universal as so. The presentation of the information is without contract or any type of guarantee assurance.

The trademarks that are used are without any consent, and the publication of the trademark is without permission or backing by the trademark owner.

All trademarks and brands within this book are for clarifying purposes only and are owned by the owners themselves, not affiliated with this document.

Table of contents

INTRODUCTION 12

CHAPTER 1: INTRODUCTION TO JAPANESE FOOD 14

1.1 History and Origin of Japanese Food 15

1.2 History of Traditional Japanese Dishes 16

1.3 Evolution of Japanese Food over Time 17

1.4 Popularity of Japanese Dishes in the U.S.A 18

CHAPTER 2: JAPANESE FOOD: HOME COOKING VS. DINE- IN EXPERIENCE 20

2.1 Difference between Home Cooking Vs. Dine-in Experience 21

2.2 Health Benefits of Japanese Food 23

2.3 Different Properties of Spices used in Japanese Food 26

CHAPTER 3: JAPANESE BREAKFAST RECIPES 30

3.1 Japanese Omelette 30

3.2 Breakfast Ramen 31

3.3 Japanese Style Pancakes 33

3.4 Japanese Breakfast Rice Bowl 34

3.5 Tamagoyaki 36

3.6 Tonkatsu 37

3.7 Japanese Egg Omelette Sandwich 38

3.8 Japanese Rolled Omelette 39

3.9 Hiroshima Okonomiyaki 40

3.10 Japanese Hibachi Style Fried Rice 42

3.11 Japanese Breakfast Skillet 43

CHAPTER 4: JAPANESE LUNCH AND DINNER RECIPES . 45

4.1 Onigiri 45

4.2 Natto 46

4.3 Agedashi Tofu 47

4.4 Nasu Dengaku 49

4.5 Omurice 50

4.6 Okonomiyaki 52

4.7 Cheesy Ramen Carbonara 53

4.8 Yakisoba 54

4.9 Baked chicken Katsu 56

4.10 Hayashi Ground Beef Curry 57

4.11 Ramen Noodle Skillet with Steak 58

4.12 Chicken Teriyaki 59

4.13 Japanese Salmon Bowl 60

4.14 Scattered Sushi Rice/Chirashi-zushi 62

4.15 Broiled Shrimp and Vegetables/ Kushiyaki 63

4.16 Chicken in a Pot/Mizutaki 64

CHAPTER 5: JAPANESE SALAD RECIPES ... 66

5.1 Japanese cucumber Salad (Sunomo) ... 66

5.2 Japanese Watercess Salad ... 67

5.3 Kani Salad ... 68

5.4 Oshitashi ... 69

5.5 Japanese Cabbage Salad ... 70

5.6 Ramen Noodle Salad ... 71

5.7 Pork Chimichurri Salad ... 72

5.8 Spring Green Salad ... 73

5.9 Japanese Corn Salad ... 74

CHAPTER 6: JAPANESE SOUP RECIPES ... 76

6.1 Miso soup ... 76

6.2 Ochazuke ... 77

6.3 Ozoni ... 78

6.4 Japanese Clear Onions Soup ... 78

6.5 Wonton Dumplings Soup ... 79

6.6 Kimchi and Tofu Soup ... 80

6.7 Shio Koji Mushroom Soup ... 81

6.8 Yudofu ... 82

6.9 Ojiya Rice Soup ... 83

6.10 Oshiruko Sweet Red Bean Soup ... 83

6.11 Bean Paste Soup ... 84

6.12 Egg Drop Soup 85

CHAPTER 7: JAPANESE SNACKS 86

7.1 Japanese Summer Sandwiches 86

7.2 Fresh Spring Rolls with Japanese Style Sauce 87

7.3 Karaage Japanese Fried Chicken 88

7.4 Tazukuri Candied Sardines 89

7.5 Kuromame Sweetened Black Soybean 90

7.6 Takoyaki Octopus Balls 92

7.7 Yakitori Grilled Skewers 93

7.8 Sweet Ginger Meatballs 94

7.9 Satsuma Age Fried Fish Cake with Vegetables 95

7.10 Sweet and Salty Nori Seaweed Popcorn 96

CHAPTER 8: JAPANESE DESSERTS 98

8.1 Kinako Dango 98

8.2 Japanese Style Pumpkin Pudding 99

8.3 Dorayaki 100

8.4 Fluffy Japanese Cheesecake 101

8.5 Matcha Ice cream 102

8.6 Taiyaki 103

8.7 Zenzai 104

8.8 Okoshi 105

8.9 Dango 106

8.10 Kasutera 106

8.11 Daifuku 107

CHAPTER 9: RAMEN AND SUSHI RECIPES 109

9.1 Shoyu Ramen 109

9.2 Miso Ramen 110

9.3 Simple Homemade Chicken Ramen 111

9.4 Vegetarian Ramen 111

9.5 Ramen Noodles 112

9.6 Pork Ramen 112

9.7 Instant Ramen 112

9.8 Sushi 113

9.9 Japanese Sushi Rolls 114

CHAPTER 10: MOST POPULAR AND ALTERNATIVE JAPANESE RECIPES 117

10.1 Sashimi 117

10.2 Unadon 118

10.3 Tempura 118

10.4 Soba 119

10.5 Udon 120

10.6 Sukiyaki 120

10.7 Oden 122

10.8 Gohan - Steamed Rice 123

10.9 Tonkatsu 123

10.10 Wagashi 124

10.11 Japanese Matcha Green Tea 125

CHAPTER 11: JAPANESE VEGETARIAN RECIPES............126

11.1 Kenchin Vegetable Soup 126

11.2 Vegan Japanese Omelette 127

11.3 Japanese Vegetable Pancake 128

11.4 Vegetarian Japanese Curry 129

11.5 Vegetable Tempura 129

11.6 Japanese Edamame 130

11.7 Japanese Eggplant Curry 131

11.8 Mushroom and Tofu Potstickers 131

11.9 Vegetable Teppanyaki 132

11.10 Naturally Sweet Red Bean Daifuku 133

11.11 Japanese Carrot Pickles 134

11.12 Mango Mochi 134

11.13 Japanese Green Avocado Salad 136

11.14 Sweet Potatoes and Avocado Green Salad 136

11.15 Japanese Baked Sweet Potato 137

11.16 Japanese Fried Rice 138

11.17 Kenchinjiru 139

CONCLUSION 141

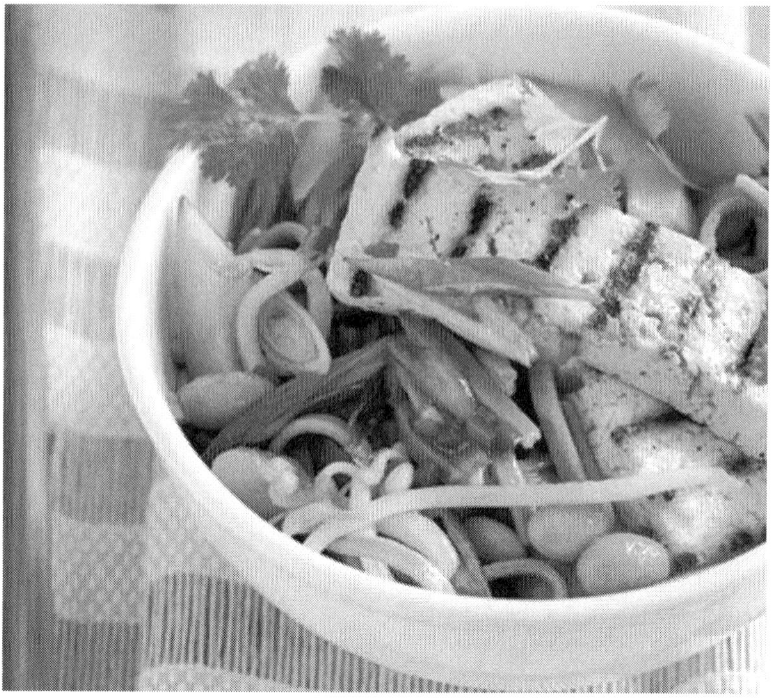

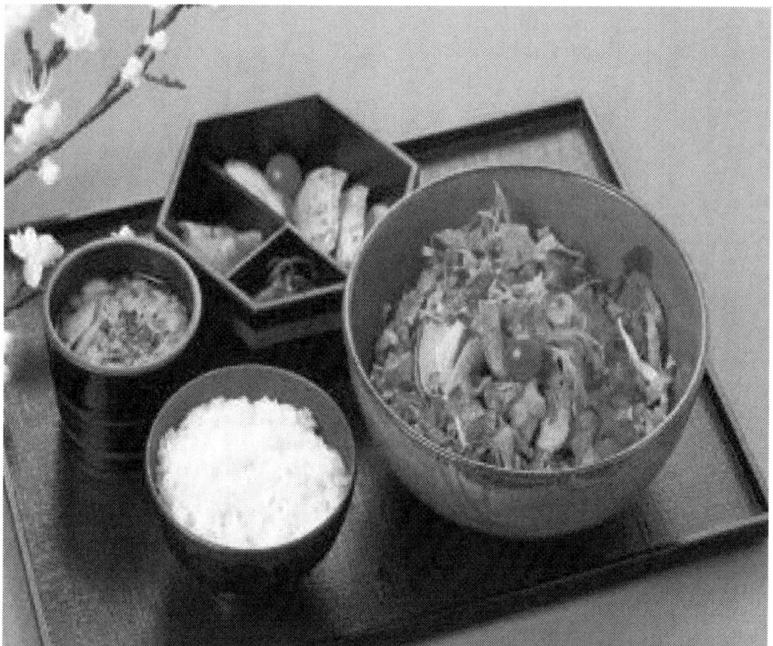

Introduction

We all love to have food conveniently. Everyone loves to order food or get to some restaurant to have their favorite dishes but eating out can be unhealthy to a greater extent. Towards the end of a busy day, eating out or ordering your food might feel like the most convenient and the most straightforward choice. In any case, comfort and restaurant prepared food can negatively affect your health and wellbeing. One of the simplest ways to improve your health is by preparing more home-cooked meals.

Our world comprises of various countries with numerous types of cuisines that are being eaten all around the globe. One such cuisine is called the Japanese cuisine that is, as the name clearly depicts, originated from the Asian country, Japan.

Japanese cooking mainly includes the territorial and conventional nourishments of Japan, which have been developed through hundreds of years of political, monetary, and social changes. The customary cooking of Japan depends on rice with miso soup and different dishes; there is an accentuation on seasonal ingredients.

In this book regarding Japanese home cooking, we will discuss in detail the history as well as the origin of Japanese food and its evolution over the passage of time. You will also get a section in the book where you will learn the reason behind the popularity of Japanese cuisine in the U.S.A. In this book, you will get the knowledge regarding the difference between home cooking and dine in experience while having Japanese food.

There are various different kinds of spices being used in Japanese cooking, out of which many have been discussed in detail in the chapters below. You will learn different recipes, including breakfast, lunch, dinner, dessert, salad, soups, snacks, sushi, alternative, and traditional as well as vegetarian recipes. All the recipes mentioned in this book are extremely easy to make all on your own at home. Now, let us not brag too much and finally start cooking Japanese at home.

Chapter 1: Introduction to Japanese Food

Japanese cooking has been around for more than 2,000 years with its strong links from both China and Korea. Although, it has just been a couple of hundreds of years since all the impacts have come to form what is now known as Japanese cuisine. Japanese cooking has overwhelmed the culinary scene. With its one-of-a-kind taste of flavors and fragile mix of sweet and savory, it is no big surprise Japanese meals are so well known. From sushi to ramen, Japanese and Japanese-motivated dishes can be found worldwide, including your own kitchen. You do not need to be a master chef to bring home the exquisite flavors of Japanese cuisine.

Japanese individuals call every supper "Gohan." For instance, breakfast is classified "asa-Gohan." A bowl of steamed rice is included for every single Japanese dinner and is very important for breakfast, lunch, or supper. Side dishes are called okazu and are presented with rice and soup. Rice is a staple of the Japanese eating routine. Rice cakes (mochi) are additionally usually very common. They range from sweet to exquisite and have various preparations from bubbled to barbecued.

1.1 History and Origin of Japanese Food

Japanese cuisine has been influenced by the food customs of other nations but has adopted and refined them to create its own unique cooking style and eating habits. The first foreign influence on Japan was China around 300 B.C. when the Japanese learned to cultivate rice. The use of chopsticks and the consumption of soy sauce and soybean curd (tofu) also came from China.

The Buddhist religion, one of the two major religions in Japan today, was another important influence on the Japanese diet. In the A.D. 700s, the rise of Buddhism led to a ban on eating meat. The popular dish sushi came about as a result of this ban. In the 1800s, cooking styles became simpler. A wide variety of vegetarian foods were served in small portions, using one of five standard cooking techniques.

Starting in the mid-1200s, trade with different nations started bringing Western-style impacts to Japan. The Dutch presented corn, potatoes, and yams. The Portuguese presented tempura. After a boycott of more than 1,000 years, hamburger got back to Japan during the Meiji Period (1868–1912). Western foods, for example, bread, espresso, and frozen yogurt gotten well known during the late 20th century.

Another Western impact has been the presentation of timesaving cooking strategies. These incorporate the electric rice cooker, bundled nourishments, for example, moment noodles, moment miso soup, and moment pickling blends. However, the Japanese are as yet dedicated to their exemplary cooking conventions. All foods were divided into five color groups (green, red, yellow, white, and black-purple) and six tastes (bitter, sour, sweet, hot, salty, and delicate). The Japanese continue to use this cooking system.

1.2 History of Traditional Japanese Dishes

Japan is a small country, but each region or even a city has its own specials. Mainly, there is the Kanto region (eastern area of the main island) food and Kansai region (western area of the main island) food. Generally, Kanto food has intense flavors, and Kansai food is lightly seasoned. Many dishes are cooked differently between the Kansai and Kanto regions.

Milk and other dairy items have neglected to appreciate a similar prominence in Europe as they do in Japan. The main Japanese dairy item known to history was delivered between the eighth and fourteenth hundred years. Cattle were often raised only for drawing carts or ploughing fields. To utilize them for meat or even for milk was, until relatively recently, a long-forgotten practice.

Pepper and cloves were known from the eighth century and were imported either by means of China or legitimately from Southeast Asia, and garlic was additionally developed, taking things down a notch. In any case, these flavors were utilized essentially to make medications and beauty care products.

In the absence of red meat, fish was an effective substitute, and as an island nation, this source of food was abundant and has influenced many of today's most famous dishes. However, before the introduction of modern delivery systems, the difficulty of preserving and transporting fresh marine fish minimized consumption in inland areas where freshwater fish were commonly eaten instead.

Preserving fish additionally got famous, and sushi started as a method for saving fish by placing it in boiled rice. Fish that are salted and set-in rice are saved by lactic corrosive maturation, which forestalls the expansion of the microbes that achieve rot. This more established sort of sushi is still delivered in the zones encompassing Lake Biwa in western Japan, and comparative sorts are likewise known in Korea, southwestern China, and Southeast Asia.

To eat Japanese-style suppers, chopsticks are usually utilized. Also, Japanese people use forks, knives, or spoons, depending on what types of food people are eating. The traditional Japanese table setting is to place a bowl of rice on your left and to place a bowl of miso soup on your right side of the table. Other dishes are set behind these bowls. Chopsticks are placed on a chopstick holder in front of soup and rice bowls.

Today, Japanese cooking is still intensely affected by the four seasons and geology. Fish and vegetables are most ordinarily eaten. While to certain westerners, the food may appear to be practically insipid, freshness, presentation, and balance of flavors to be of paramount importance.

1.3 Evolution of Japanese Food over Time

A significant part of the rice devoured by Japan was imported from other Eastern nations, so once the trade stopped, the rice flexibly dwindled. To additional the issue, returnees from combat areas just as U.S. occupation in Japan raised the populace to numbers higher than those of pre-war levels. Helpless rice harvests in 1944 and 1945 because of climate and war compounded the criticalness of the circumstance, bringing about broad hunger and starvation, especially among youngsters.

This suffering, however, ended up having a silver lining. During the U.S. occupation of Japan following World War II, the United States government supplied Japan with large quantities of wheat flour to rehabilitate the Japanese economy as a strategic move during the cold war. This wheat flour served as a substitute for rice, and was used mainly to make wheat noodles for Chinese noodle soup at the time referred to as shina soba or chuka soba. This noodle soup is often sold in Japanese black markets from yatai or small food carts, which later became known as ramen.

The daily diet of the Japanese people has changed drastically over the past years, with corresponding changes in agricultural production. In the early post-war years of food shortage, people ate sweet potatoes, barley, and millet more than white rice, which was scarce and expensive. Vegetables and fish in small quantities served as side dishes.

Although rice regained its traditional place at the center of the preferred Japanese diet by the early 1950s, western staples of meat, bread, and dairy products soon made inroads. Many people credit the national school lunch program with changing the diet preferences of the younger generation because it served milk and a roll along with a hot dish.

Japanese now eat much more meat, bread, and dairy products, while consumption of rice has declined. By the 1970s, western style restaurants and fast foods further changed the eating habits of urban Japanese. Instead of the traditional diet of rice for breakfast and dinner and noodles for lunch, most urban Japanese now eat a western breakfast and lunch, with rice remaining the staple food only for most dinners.

1.4 Popularity of Japanese Dishes in the U.S.A

Japanese food is getting more mainstream, alongside a developing movement towards sound reasoning. The quantity of Japanese cafés is developing, even in America. While the taste is a reason for the popularity, the colorful plating of items that allow for dishes to also be enjoyed visually is another.

After Italian, Chinese, and Mexican, Japanese food is presumably the most mainstream ethnic cooking in the United

States. Before 1970 only a few big cities, and a few Japanese-American communities in Hawaii and California, had Japanese restaurants; the foods, and the manners and customs, attracted few mainstream American diners. The popularity of sushi would change all that. While Americanised sushi variations like the ever-popular California roll made the form popular, once introduced to sushi, Americans began to crave it, even if it meant eating raw fish.

However, real Japanese food is available and popular at restaurants all over the United States of America. Restaurants will, naturally, avoid many Japanese foods that will never appeal to American taste: the pungent, sticky fermented soy paste called natto is a perfect example, although even this is available in Japanese groceries.

A real Japanese restaurant has a staff of Japanese chefs. Good Japanese cooking is subtle and takes a long time to master. Sushi chefs are particularly highly trained and are skilled at avoiding health issues when dealing with raw seafood. A number of pan-Asian restaurants offer Japanese food in combination with Chinese or Korean food. The Japanese dishes at these restaurants should be reliable if prepared by a genuine Japanese chef.

Thirty years ago, the typical Japanese restaurant served a little of everything. Now Japanese food is so popular that the market supports numerous specialties eating concepts such as the famous sushi, tempura, shabu yautia, udon and soba, ramen, teriyaki, bento box, nabe, yakiniku, sukiyaki, and donburi.

Chapter 2: Japanese Food: Home Cooking Vs. Dine- in Experience

Japanese cooking incorporates the local and conventional nourishments of Japan, which have created through hundreds of years of political, financial, and social changes. The customary cooking of Japan depends on rice with miso soup and different dishes; there is an emphasis on seasonal ingredients. Side dishes often consist of fish, pickled vegetables, and vegetables cooked in broth.

Seafood is common, often grilled, but also served raw as sashimi or in sushi. Seafood and vegetables are also deep-fried in a light batter, as tempura. Apart from rice, staples include noodles, such as soba and udon. Japan also has many simmered dishes such as fish products in broth called oden, or beef in sukiyaki and nikujaga.

2.1 Difference between Home Cooking Vs. Dine-in Experience

While many restaurants and fast-food outlets offer us convincing marketing statements that they offer healthy and nutritional food, studies frequently find that this is not the case. The sugar and sodium substance of most handled foods cause them to be not kidding dangers to our wellbeing. These are likewise similar characteristics which permit these foods to get addictive. The eatery business supports overconsumption and extravagance in foods that we know to be undesirable for our bodies.

Neither is restaurant food as healthy for us as what we would make at home. At the same time, the cost of eating out puts a large strain on many of our food budgets. Cooking at home is the best choice for having a consistently healthy, budget-friendly diet.

Individuals all around the globe are occupied with work, school and other additional exercises. Nobody actually has the opportunity to cook, so families are continually going out to eat at an eatery. At the point when a family eats at home, they, will pay not as much as cafés in light of the fact that when they purchase food from the market they purchase for better quality and a superior cost. It is very simple. There is most likely even a not insignificant rundown of advantages that a considerable lot of you previously experienced eating at home yourselves. Following are the differences between home cooking and dine-in experience:

1. **You can save money.**

In the long run, preparing meals at home may save you money. A group of fundamental ingredients frequently comes in at a lower sticker price than a single restaurant dish.

You can likewise wind up getting more suppers out of a formula you make at home than if you request takeout, or have extras to take to work the following day. After only a couple weeks, you could see perceptible reserve funds begin to accumulate.

2. **Keep up calorie count.**

The average fast food order ranges between 1,100 to 1,200 calories total that is almost all of a woman's recommended daily calorie intake (1,600 to 2,400 calories) and almost two thirds of a man's daily intake (2,000 to 3,000 calories). Furthermore, if you think independent cafés, and modest chains do any better, reconsider. Making a meal yourself means you can make sure the portion sizes and calorie counts are where you want them to be. Recipes often come with nutritional information and serving size suggestions, which makes that even easier.

3. **It is fun to cook.**

At the point when you are making a meal without any preparation, you will find and explore different avenues regarding various ingredients, flavours, and foods. And as with any activity, the more time you spend in the kitchen, the better you become at creating fantastic meals. You would be missing out this fun if you would keep on ordering your food or going for dine-in to any restaurant.

4. **Save plenty of time.**

Part of ordering take-out means waiting for the food to arrive or driving to get it. Depending on where you live, what time you order, and whether or not the delivery person is good with directions, this could actually take more time than if you would simply make a meal at home.

Cooking at home does not have to take a lot of time if you do not want it to.

By using different services, you eliminate the need to look for recipes or grocery shop. Everything you need comes right to your door; in the exact pre-portioned amounts you will be using.

5. **You will feel healthy**

Some research specialists recommend that individuals that more frequently prepare food themselves, instead of getting a take-out meal, have a generally more beneficial eating regimen. These examinations additionally give us the idea that café suppers ordinarily contain higher measures of sodium, immersed fat, absolute fat, and large number of calories than home-prepared meals. While cooking without anyone else at home you have full scale authority over what is going in your food. That can improve things fundamentally to your overall prosperity.

6. **More family times.**

Cooking together can offer you an event to reconnect with your assistant just as loved ones. Cooking has various favourable circumstances as well. The American Psychological Association communicates that trying new things together like learning another formula together can help keep a couple related and busy with their relationship.

The most important fact is that food simply tastes better when it is been prepared in home rather than any restaurant. Thus, it is smarter to cook home and eat well instead of taking off to an eatery only because of your apathetic daily schedule.

2.2 Health Benefits of Japanese Food

The Japanese eating regimen depends on the rule of wellbeing and life span. Japanese food is not just elegant and mouth-watering yet additionally offers different medical advantages.

Japanese food generally comprises of natural ingredients, refined sugar or other food sources, and high measures of grains and vegetables. Following are a portion of the numerous medical advantages of appreciating Japanese food:

1. **Large variety of fruits and vegetables.**

The Japanese eating regimen comprises of a wide scope of vegetables, which contains fundamental minerals to help generally sustenance. For instance, kelp is profoundly nutritious, including a lot of iodine that can enable your body to save a sound thyroid. Likewise, high measures of organic product are burned-through for breakfast and treat, which has high measures of fibre and water content.

2. **Healthy drinks.**

Japanese eateries generally incorporate green tea with their suppers, which have various medical advantages. Green tea is known to help direct pulse, lower glucose, support the safe framework, lower cholesterol, and hinder the maturing cycle. It likewise contains a large portion of the measure of caffeine that espresso does, and assists breaks with bringing down oils in your stomach related framework. Green tea additionally makes a loose and centred mental perspective because of it being wealthy in cancer prevention agents.

3. **Reduced risk of various cancers.**

Japan has had an extremely low risk for hormone-dependent cancers such as breast and prostate cancers. This is attributed to the high consumption of vegetables, fruits, healthy fats, high-fibre foods, and overall lower calorie intake.

4. **Lower chances of cardiac diseases.**

Japan has one of the lowest rates for the development of heart disease in the world and even more compared to developed countries. The reasoning behind these low instances of heart diseases is that the Japanese diet is filled with foods that help improve heart health.

Furthermore, Japanese food lacks ingredients in their diet which promotes poor cardiac health like high levels of saturated fats, modified carbohydrates from processed foods, and lower levels of sugar consumption. Soy is commonly in many Japanese dishes, and it is known to decrease the risk of heart attacks, as well as, regulate blood pressure. The Japanese use soy as an alternative to red meat, which can be very high in saturated fats.

5. **High amount of protein.**

The Japanese culture comprehends that eating excellent wellsprings of protein advances a more advantageous way of life. A significant number of the dishes in Japanese food are brimming with protein, which is staggeringly helpful to your body. Fish, chicken, and even tofu are probably the most widely recognized staples in Japanese food. When you eat a lot of protein, you create stronger building blocks for your bones, your muscles, your cartilage, your skin, and even your blood.

Protein also provides large amounts of iron, which keeps your blood oxygenated, so it continues to flow through your body as efficiently as possible. Likewise, the Japanese eating regimen utilizes a ton of fish rather than red meats since it brings down the dangers of coronary episodes. By consuming more fish, you are also gaining a great source of omega 3 fatty acids and brain-boosting nutrients.

The traditional Japanese diet combines simple soups, steamed rice or noodles, fish, seafood, tofu or natto, and a variety of minimally processed sides. The traditional Japanese diet focuses on whole, minimally processed, nutrient-rich, seasonal foods. It is particularly rich in seafood, vegetables, and fruit, and limits meat, dairy, and snacks. It may improve digestion, aid weight management, help you live longer, and protect against various diseases.

2.3 Different Properties of Spices used in Japanese Food

Spices are utilized for flavor and for stylish allure in Japanese cooking. Probably the most widely recognized are: shiso, akajiso, mistuba, kaiware, sancho, and chrysanthemum leaves. Shichimi Togarashi is the most famous flavoring other than soy sauce.

1. **Mitsuba.**

Mitsuba is a tasty kind of parsley with a fresh surface and an invigorating fragrance. Added as an exquisite embellishment to flavorful custard dishes, soups, and sashimi, it is likewise southern style entire in tempura or added to plates of mixed greens. Mitsuba can be utilized at whatever point more grounded tasting parsley is required.

2. **Akajiso**

Akajiso or red shiso is also used to dye pickled plums red. These umeboshi are used throughout Japanese cuisine as a garnish or as a flavoring in sauces, dressings, rice balls and other dishes. A specialty gin made in Kyoto is made from red shiso and flavoured with yusu, sansho pepper, and juniper berries. This gin which is lighter than its western counterpart has a smooth but complex flavor.

3. **Sansho**

Sansho is a pretty herb with a dainty balanced design that is a good seasoning for soups and fish dishes, in particular eel specialties or chicken. With its refreshing mint like flavor, sansho is a popular herb enhancer in Japan. Apart from its leaf, the seed pods of the sansho plant give a tingling dimension to eel or chicken dishes; its flavor is lemony and peppery and can deliver a flavorful punch.

4. **Yuzu Koshu**

Japan's local specialty spice, yuzu kosho, is made of the peel of the Asian citrus yuzu, salt, and chili pepper. You can commonly find it as a tube or jar of yellow paste in Japanese supermarkets. Traditionally used in nabe, or Japanese hotpot, yuzu kosho also pairs wonderfully with miso, tonkatsu (fried pork cutlet), yakitori (grilled meat skewers), sashimi, and all manner of Japanese noodle dishes.

5. **Ponzu**

Ponzu is the citrus sauce that even those who hate citrus will love. Made from the juice of any citrus fruit, soy sauce, mirin (rice wine), and dashi (Japanese soup stock), this tangy vinaigrette like sauce can brighten the flavor of your gyoza, stir-fry, marinated meats, and tofu dishes.

6. **Chrysanthemum**

Although somewhat bitter in taste, chrysanthemum leaves are often added to hot pot dishes and stir fries. The buds and flowers are infused to make a celebratory herbal tea served on special occasions like weddings.

7. **Wasabi**

In case you are acquainted with any topping on this rundown, it is most likely wasabi. Wasabi is notable for being the threateningly hot green glue that goes with sushi, verifiably thought to have restorative properties when eaten with crude fish. Yet, you can likewise utilize it to decorate soba noodles, or even make a wasabi dressing for sushi bowls and cooked fish.

8. Shichimi Togarashi

Shichimi togarashi is a flavorful mixture of sansho, hemp seeds, ground nori, black and white sesame seeds, white poppy seeds, ground chilies, shiso, and ginger and dried tangerine peel. These ingredients vary according to the region, but basically it is a zesty chili powder used to flavor Udon. This popular seven spice seasoning originated in the 1600s when chilies were first introduced to Japan and has been enjoyed ever since as a seasoning for udon, ramen, hot pot, and chicken dishes.

9. Rayu

Commonly found in Japanese-style Chinese food, rayu is chili oil made with sesame oil, garlic, ginger, onion, spices, and sometimes sesame seeds. You may have seen this signature red oil available at the tables of most ramen shops. It also serves as a great dipping sauce for meals and can spice up any regular bowl of rice, noodles, or tofu.

10. Kaiware

Kaiware is a type of radish sprout with a hot, peppery flavor like watercress. Useful as a spicy garnish, it is excellent in sandwiches, stir fries, salads and sushi. Often it is sprinkled on top of tuna or beef tataki to give a peppery accent to the other ingredients.

11. Shiso

Shiso consists of large aromatic leaves, either purple or green, with a refreshing scent and flavor. When served raw with sushi or sashimi, shiso is said to prevent food poisoning because of its antiseptic or antibacterial qualities. Other medicinal characteristics include anti-inflammatory powers with illnesses such as allergies, colds, and arthritis.

Otherwise, shiso leaves are used as a garnish for sashimi, wrapped around onigiri, used to flavor pickled plums, deep fried in tempura batter, or added to rice dishes.

Shiso is also a refreshing herb to add to salads, egg sandwiches, or in sauces such as pesto or gremolata. Very easy to grow in pots on your patio, shiso will grow waist high and propagate easily if the conditions are right.

12. Furikake

Furikake is a broad term that applies to any dry Japanese spices made to be sprinkled over cooked rice. Common varieties might include salmon flakes, bits of dried omelet, sesame seeds, wasabi, seaweed flakes, bonito flakes, and nearly any other Japanese seasoning you can think of! You can try out special prefectural varieties, or simply stick with safe old seaweed flavor to spice up your rice, noodles, fried chicken, or salads.

13. Aonori

Aonori, or dried seaweed flakes, are a ubiquitous Japanese seasoning that lends its familiar earthy flavor to much of Japanese cuisine. Traditionally, it goes atop takoyaki, okonomiyaki, and yakisoba.

You will discover a great deal of these fixings in standard Japanese cooking, so unquestionably adventure outside your customary range of familiarity with some conventional and extraordinary Japanese dishes. In any case, the beautiful universe of Japanese flavors and sauces additionally has a lot of space for experimentation.

Chapter 3: Japanese Breakfast Recipes

Rather than the sweet oats or additionally filling bacon and egg dishes that fill in as the cornerstone of numerous American breakfast menus, Japanese morning meals centre on pungent, appetizing flavours that fulfil and empower you for the afternoon. The components of this hearty-yet-not-too-filling breakfast might seem more like lunch or dinner to Americans, and that is by design. Following are some amazing Japanese breakfast recipes:

3.1 Japanese Omelette

Cooking Time: 5 minutes

Serving Size: 1

Ingredients:
- Soy sauce, one tbsp.
- Eggs, four
- Sugar, one tbsp.
- Mirin, one tbsp.

- Salt, as required
- Cooking oil, as required

Method:
1. First, beat your eggs well in a bowl using either a fork, or chopsticks if you are an expert chopstick user.
2. Add one tablespoon each of soy sauce, mirin and sugar and a little salt to your mix.
3. Put a small amount of cooking oil in your pan and bring it up to medium heat. Keep some kitchen roll handy to help keep the pan oiled during cooking.
4. Add a small amount of your egg mix into the heated pan. Once the egg is cooked slightly so that the top is still slightly uncooked, push it over to the side of your pan.
5. Add a little more oil to the pan using the kitchen roll and add another small amount of the egg mix to your pan.
6. You can then begin to roll the first bit of egg over the mix you just put in the pan until you have a small roll of egg.
7. Continue adding a small amount of egg while oiling the pan each time in between.
8. Your omelette is now done so remove from the pan and wait to cool before slicing it up into thin pieces with a sharp knife.
9. Your dish is ready to be served.

3.2 Breakfast Ramen

Cooking Time: 25 minutes

Serving Size: 6

Ingredients:
- Sage leaves, a bunch
- Unsalted butter, a quarter cup
- Bacon, eight strips
- Enki mushrooms, a bunch
- Miso soup, two cups
- Broth, twelve cups
- Poached eggs, six
- Ramen noodles, six cups
- Tomato, one
- Salt, as required
- Cooking oil, as required
- Avocado, one

Method:
1. Preheat oven to 400 degrees. Lay a piece of parchment paper on a baking sheet.
2. Spread the bacon strips on the sheet and bake for about twenty minutes. Watch carefully as time will vary with ovens. They will crisp up with no need to turn the pieces over. Save your bacon grease in a jar because you can use it to make the ramen soup bases. Remove from the oven and set on a paper towel.
3. Heat the butter in a small skillet over high heat until the butter starts to brown. Immediately scatter the sage leaves in the pan and cook for about 10 seconds.
4. Boil a pot of water for your noodles. In a separate saucepan, bring two cups miso base, and twelve cups

(2.8 L) of broth to a boil, then lower the heat and let it simmer until it is ready to be served.

5. Boil the noodles. If fresh, boil for about one minute, if packaged, boil for about two minutes. As soon as they are done, drain well and separate into serving bowls.
6. Pour two cups of soup over each bowl of noodles.
7. Top each bowl with mushrooms, avocado slices, tomatoes, poached egg, a crumbled up half strip of bacon, and crispy sage; lay another whole piece of bacon on the side.
8. Drizzle the browned butter over the top for added flavour.
9. You dish is ready to be served.

3.3 Japanese Style Pancakes

Cooking Time: 40 minutes

Serving Size: 4

Ingredients:
- Milk, one and a half cup
- Baking powder, two tsp.
- Sugar, three tbsp.
- Kosher salt, half tsp.
- Unsalted butter, four tbsp.
- Eggs, four
- Vanilla extract, one tsp.
- Cream of tartar, a quarter tsp.
- Maple syrup, as required

- All-purpose flour, one and a half cup

Method:
1. Whisk together the flour, sugar, baking powder and salt in a large bowl.
2. Whisk together the milk, melted butter, vanilla and egg yolk in a medium bowl until combined.
3. Beat the egg whites and cream of tartar in another large bowl with an electric mixer on medium-high speed until stiff peaks form, about two minutes.
4. Stir the milk mixture into the flour mixture until just combined. Then gently fold in the remaining egg whites until just combined.
5. Coat a large non-stick skillet with non-stick cooking spray and heat over medium-low heat.
6. Put the prepared ring moulds in the middle of the skillet and fill each with half cup of batter.
7. Cover the skillet with the lid and cook until the batter rises to the tops of the ring moulds and is golden on the bottom for about five minutes.
8. Release the bottom of the pancakes with a spatula. Grasp the sides of the ring moulds with tongs to stabilize them and then carefully flip.
9. Cover and cook until golden on the other side, about five minutes more. Transfer to a plate and remove the mould.
10. Serve with butter and maple syrup.

3.4 Japanese Breakfast Rice Bowl

Cooking Time: 3 minutes

Serving Size: 1

Ingredients:
- Egg, one
- Thinly sliced nori, as required
- Hondashi, a pinch
- Mirin, half tsp.
- Soy sauce, half tsp.
- MSG, a pinch
- Furikake, as required
- Cooked white rice, one cup

Method:
1. Place rice in a bowl and make a shallow scoop in the centre.
2. Break the whole egg into the centre.
3. Season with half teaspoon soy sauce, a pinch of salt, a pinch of MSG, half teaspoon mirin, and a pinch of Hondashi.
4. Stir vigorously with chopsticks to incorporate egg; it should become pale yellow, frothy, and fluffy in texture.
5. Taste and adjust seasonings as necessary.
6. Sprinkle with furikake and nori, make a small scoop in the top, and add the other egg yolk.
7. Your dish is ready to be served.

3.5 Tamagoyaki

Cooking Time: 10 minutes

Serving Size: 2

Ingredients:

- Eggs, three
- Olive oil, one tsp.
- Shirodashi, two tsp.
- Salt, pinch
- Water, two tbsp.

Method:

1. Crack the eggs into a medium size mixing bowl.
2. Add seasoning and mix them all together gently to avoid too much bubble forming.
3. Strain the egg mixture through a sieve a few times.
4. Pour about two tbsp. oil in a small bowl and soak kitchen paper and set aside.
5. Heat two tsp. olive oil in the frying pan over medium heat till you can feel the heat when you hover your hand over the pan.
6. Pour a quarter of egg mixture into the pan.
7. Break any bubbles that have been formed with the edge of the chopsticks and scramble gently and slightly.
8. When the surface is solidified a little, fold and push the egg to one end of the pan with chopsticks.
9. Repeat the procedure and make an egg roll.
10. Your dish is ready to be served.

3.6 Tonkatsu

Cooking Time: 10 minutes

Serving Size: 4

Ingredients:

- Eggs, two
- Flour, as required
- Tonkatsu sauce, for serving
- Shredded Napa cabbage, as required
- Bread crumbs, as required
- Pork loins, four pieces
- Oil, for frying
- Salt, pinch
- Pepper, as required

Method:

1. Pound to flatten the loin cutlet to about a quarter inch. Salt and pepper both sides of each cutlet.
2. Dredge each in flour, then dip into beaten eggs and press into bread crumbs to coat both sides.
3. Heat a large skillet with about half inch of oil until hot.
4. Lay the cutlets in the hot oil. Deep-fry until golden brown, about five minutes, turning them once or twice.
5. Drain the cutlets on paper towels and cut the pork into bite-size strips that can be eaten with chopsticks.
6. Arrange the pork on a platter lined with the shredded cabbage, and garnish with lemon wedges.

7. Serve the sauce on the side for dipping, or pour it over the pork and cabbage.

3.7 Japanese Egg Omelette Sandwich

Cooking Time: 5 minutes

Serving Size: 2

Ingredients:

- Eggs, two
- Japanese soup stock, half tsp.
- Hot water, one tsp.
- Soy sauce, one tsp.
- Mayonnaise, as required
- Bread slices, four
- Oil, for frying
- Salt, pinch
- Pepper, as required

Method:

1. Melt the Japanese soup stock in hot water, and keep it cool.
2. Mix all ingredients using a whisk.
3. Put oil thinly to a 12 cm × 12 cm heat-resistant container.
4. Wrap the container and warm one minute thirty seconds with microwave.
5. Take it out and keep it cool. Wipe off extra moisture with kitchen paper.

6. Spread the mayonnaise over one side of breads. Put on omelette and cut it into four pieces.
7. Your dish is ready to be served.

3.8 Japanese Rolled Omelette

Cooking Time: 10 minutes

Serving Size: 4

Ingredients:
- Eggs, six
- Daikon, for serving
- Soy sauce, one tsp.
- Salt, one tsp.
- Mirin, one tbsp.
- Caster sugar, one tbsp.
- Shiso leaves, as required
- Oil, for frying

Method:
1. Mix the dashi stock with mirin, sugar, soy sauce, and salt.
2. Add to the beaten eggs and stir well. Heat the omelette pan over medium heat.
3. Pour in some egg mixture and tilt the pan to coat evenly.
4. When the omelette starts to set, roll it up towards you, using a pair of chopsticks or a spatula.
5. Keep the rolled omelette in the pan and push it back to the farthest side from you.

6. Again, pour in some egg mixture into the empty side, lift up the first roll with chopsticks and let the egg mixture runs underneath.
7. When it looks half set, roll the omelette around the first roll to make a single roll with many layers.
8. Repeat the process until all egg mixture is used up.
9. Move the roll gently onto a sushi rolling mat covered with a clear sheet of plastic wrap.
10. Roll the omelette firmly into the mat and leave to sushi rolled for five minutes.
11. Grate the daikon with a daikon grater or with a very fine grater.
12. Cut the rolled omelette into one-inch slices crossways. Lay the shiso leaves on a plate and place a few pieces of omelette on top.
13. Put a small heap of grated daikon to one side and add and serve.

3.9 Hiroshima Okonomiyaki

Cooking Time: 30 minutes

Serving Size: 2

Ingredients:

- Water, two tbsps.
- Eggs, three
- Bacon, six strips
- Cabbage, 150g
- Okonomiyaki flour, half cup
- Okonomiyaki sauce, two tbsp.

- Spring onions, as required
- Bonito flakes, as required
- Yakisoba noodles, two cups
- Pickled ginger, one tsp.
- Oil, for frying
- Aonori seaweed, as required

Method:

1. Begin by chopping your green onion and cabbage. Try to chop your cabbage as finely as possible.
2. Grab a bowl and mix the okonomiyaki flour with the water, and one egg until you have a smooth batter with no lumps.
3. Now the fun part, take a frying pan or hot plate, and grease with a splash of vegetable oil and place on a medium heat.
4. Make sure the pan is evenly heated before the next step or the okonomiyaki will be difficult to be shaped.
5. Add just under half the batter to the pan in a nice even circle, remember not to make the circle too wide otherwise it will not be able to keep its shape.
6. Next, add half of the cabbage and half of the bean sprouts on top of the batter, before adding a layer of bacon.
7. Pour one tbsp. of the batter on the top of the mix to hold everything together and let the okonomiyaki cook for about ten minutes before flipping it over with a spatula to cook on the other side.
8. Grab another pan and cook one serving of yakisoba with a bit of vegetable oil and the sauce provided in the packet.

9. Once the yakisoba is cooked, with a spatula move the okonomiyaki on top of the noodles.
10. Crack an egg in a bowl and break the yolk before pouring in the first pan to the side of the okonomiyaki.
11. Place the okonomiyaki over the egg and leave to cook for two minutes.
12. Once done, flip the completed okonomiyaki over onto a plate and smother in a criss-cross pattern with okonomiyaki sauce and mayonnaise.
13. The final touch is to sprinkle the spring onion, aonori seaweed, katsuobushi and pickled ginger on the top.

3.10 Japanese Hibachi Style Fried Rice

Cooking Time: 20 minutes

Serving Size: 4

Ingredients:
- Toasted sesame oil, one tbsp.
- Salt, as required
- Ground black pepper, as required
- Eggs, two
- Cooked rice, four cups
- Soy sauce, two tbsp.
- Chopped onion, one
- Butter, four tbsp.

Method:
1. Heat a wok or large skillet over medium-high heat.

2. In a small bowl, lightly whisk together the eggs, salt, and ground black pepper.//
3. Add one tablespoon of butter into the heated wok or skillet. Once the butter melts, add in the eggs and scramble until they are no longer thin but still a soft scramble.
4. Carefully remove the cooked eggs from the skillet or wok back into the small bowl. Set aside.
5. Add in another one tablespoon of butter into the heated wok or skillet. Once the butter melts, add in the chopped onion and move around in the pan until the onion is lightly coated with the butter. Allow the onion to continue to cook until it becomes translucent.
6. Add in the remaining two tablespoons of butter into the wok or skillet along with the cooked onion. Once it melts add in the cooked rice.
7. Add in the soy sauce and toasted sesame oil with the rice. Stir the rice frequently, breaking it up as needed. Once the fried rice has been heated thoroughly and has also lightly browned, add in the egg and stir to evenly distribute.
8. Serve warm with some yum sauce.

3.11 Japanese Breakfast Skillet

Cooking Time: 20 minutes

Serving Size: 2

Ingredients:

- Japanese sweet potato, half cup
- Sliced carrots, half cup
- Fresh ginger, half tsp.

- Mirin, a quarter cup
- Sliced mushrooms, one cup
- Tamari, two tbsp.
- White onions, half cup
- Sesame oil, two tbsp.
- Organic tempeh, one block
- Vegetable broth, two cups

Method:

1. In a medium pot that will fit the block of tempeh, combine the tempeh and the vegetable broth and bring to a boil.
2. Immediately reduce to heat and simmer gently for fifteen minutes. When done, dice into small cubes and set aside.
3. In a large skillet, warm the oil and then add the diced potatoes and sliced carrots. Adjust heat to medium high and cook for fifteen minutes until the vegetables have a nice, golden color to them.
4. Add in the onions and tempeh and continue sautéing for about three minutes.
5. Add the cabbage, garlic, ginger and mushrooms, then give it a quick stir. The pan should be very dry.
6. Now deglaze with the mirin and tamari.
7. Stir for a few minutes to coat everything in the glaze.
8. Your dish is ready to be served.

All the recipes mentioned above are very easy to make at home.

Chapter 4: Japanese Lunch and Dinner Recipes

If you are an accomplished home cook or new to cooking, Japanese food is a delectable food to prepare at home. This rundown of essential Japanese plans is an extraordinary beginning stage for learning to cook all by yourself. It is useful to know the Japanese food technique. When you ace these, you can go for more complicated plans and procedures.

4.1 Onigiri

Cooking Time: 20 minutes

Serving Size: 3

Ingredients:

- Nori sheet, as required
- Umeboshi, one
- Soy sauce, half tsp.

- Mirin, half tsp.
- Tuna, one cup
- Japanese mayonnaise, two tbsp.
- Salted salmon, one piece
- Cooked rice, two cups

Method:
1. Cook the rice according to your rice cooker or if you do not have a rice cooker, follow the instructions here.
2. Transfer the cooked rice to a separate bowl to cool it down.
3. Prepare all the fillings that you are going to use and set aside.
4. Prepare seaweed sheet.
5. Place cling wrap over a rice bowl.
6. Place some of the cooked rice over the centre of the cling wrap.
7. Put about 1tsp of umeboshi on the centre of the rice then cover with the rice around.
8. Wrap the cling wrap over the rice and squeeze and mould the rice into a triangle shape with your hands.
9. Remove the cling wrap and cover the bottom of the rice triangle with a nori sheet.
10. Your dish is ready to be served.

4.2 Natto

Cooking Time: 20 minutes

Serving Size: 1

Ingredients:

- Scallions, for garnish
- Natto, one tbsp.
- Soy sauce, half tsp.
- Saikkyo, one and a half tsp.
- Tofu, half block
- Miso, two tbsp.
- Wakame seeds, a handful
- Dashi, two cups

Method:

1. Bring the dashi to a simmer in a soup pot and place the spoonful of natto into the liquid. Simmer for two minutes.
2. Place the miso pastes into the pot and use the back of a spoon to dissolve the pastes into the dashi.
3. Add the wakame and the tofu and simmer for 30 seconds longer.
4. Garnish with scallions.
5. Serve immediately.

4.3 Agedashi Tofu

Cooking Time: 20 minutes

Serving Size: 3

Ingredients:

- Flavoured oil, three cups
- Corn starch, four tbsp.

- Soy sauce, two tbsp.
- Katsuobishi, as required
- Tofu, one block
- Mirin, two tbsp.
- Daikon radish, as required
- Scallions, as required
- Shichimi Togarashi, a handful
- Dashi, one cup

Method:
1. Gather all the ingredients.
2. Wrap the tofu with three layers of paper towels and place another plate on top. Drain the water out of tofu for fifteen minutes.
3. Peel and grate the daikon and gently squeeze water out. Cut the green onion into thin slices.
4. Put dashi, soy sauce, and mirin in a small saucepan and bring to boil.
5. Remove the tofu from paper towels and cut it into eight pieces.
6. Coat the tofu with potato starch, leaving excess flour, and immediately deep fry until they turn light brown and crispy.
7. Remove the tofu and drain excess oil on a plate lined with paper towels or wire rack.
8. To serve, place the tofu in a serving bowl and gently pour the sauce without wetting the tofu.
9. Garnish with grated daikon, green onion, katsuobushi, and shichimi togarashi.

4.4 Nasu Dengaku

Cooking Time: 30 minutes

Serving Size: 4

Ingredients:
- Japanese eggplant, three
- Flavoured oil, one tbsp.
- Sake, two tbsp.
- Sugar, two tbsp.
- Miso, four tbsp.
- Sesame seeds, as required
- Tofu, one block
- Mirin, two tbsp.
- Daikon radish, three
- Konnyaku, a handful

Method:
1. Combine sake, mirin, sugar, and miso in a saucepan.
2. Mix well to combine and then bring to a gentle simmer over the lowest heat. Stir constantly and cook for few minutes.
3. When the miso is thickened, it is ready to use.
4. Use the miso glaze to slather on the foods you prepare below.
5. Wrap the tofu with two sheets of paper towel and press the tofu between two plates for 30 minutes.
6. Once the tofu is dried, cut it into small bite-sized pieces.

7. Cut the eggplant in half lengthwise and cut it in a crisscross pattern. This will help the eggplant absorb more flavors.

8. Immediately soak in water to prevent the eggplants from changing colors, and to remove the bitter taste. Drain and dry with a paper towel.

9. Place the tofu and eggplants on a rimmed baking sheet lined with parchment paper or silicone baking sheet. With a brush, apply vegetable oil on top and bottom of tofu and eggplants.

10. Bake at 400 degrees for twenty minutes, or until the eggplant is tender. Transfer the baking sheet to the working surface.

11. Meanwhile, carefully spoon some of the miso glaze onto your tofu and eggplants and spread evenly. Broil for five minutes, or until the top has nice char and caramelization.

12. Transfer to a serving platter, sprinkle with sesame seeds and serve immediately.

4.5 Omurice

Cooking Time: 20 minutes

Serving Size: 2

Ingredients:
- Boneless chicken, one pound
- Olive oil, one tbsp.
- Mixed vegetables, half cup
- Salt and pepper, as required
- Cooked Japanese rice, one and a half cup

- Soy sauce, one tsp.
- Ketchup, one tbsp.
- Milk, two tbsp.
- Eggs, two
- Cheese, a handful

Method:
1. Gather all the ingredients.
2. Chop the onion finely.
3. Cut the chicken.
4. Heat the oil in a non-stick pan and sauté the onion until softened.
5. Add the chicken and cook until no longer pink.
6. Add the mixed vegetables and season with salt and pepper.
7. Add the rice and break into small pieces.
8. Add ketchup and soy sauce and combine everything evenly with a spatula. Transfer the fried rice to a plate and wash the pan.
9. We will make the omelette one at a time. Whisk the egg and milk in a small bowl.
10. Heat the olive oil in the pan over medium high heat.
11. When the pan is hot, pour the egg mixture into the pan and tilt to cover the bottom of the pan. Lower the heat when the bottom of the egg is set.
12. Put the cheese and the divided fried rice on top of the omelette.

13. Use the spatula to fold both sides of omelette toward the middle to cover the fried rice. Slowly move the omurice to the edge of the pan.
14. Hold a plate in one hand and the pan in the other hand flip the pan and move the omurice to the plate.
15. While it is still hot, cover the omurice with a paper towel and shape it. Drizzle the ketchup on top for decoration.

4.6 Okonomiyaki

Cooking Time: 30 minutes

Serving Size: 4

Ingredients:
- Dashi, one cup
- Oyster sauce, one tbsp.
- Nagaimo, as required
- Salt, as required
- Flour one and a half cup
- Sugar, half tsp.
- Baking powder, half tsp.
- Sliced pork belly, half pound
- Milk, two tbsp.
- Eggs, four
- Cabbage, one

Method:
1. Mix all the batter ingredients.
2. Peel and grate nagaimo in a small bowl.

3. Add the grated nagaimo and dashi in the bowl.
4. Mix all together till combined. Cover the bowl with plastic wrap and let it rest in the refrigerator for at least an hour.
5. Cut the pork belly slices in half and set aside.
6. Take out the batter from the refrigerator and add eggs, tempura scraps, and pickled red ginger in the bowl. Mix well until well-combined.
7. Add chopped cabbage to the batter. Mix well before adding the rest.
8. In a large pan, heat vegetable oil on medium heat. Spread the batter evenly. If you are new to making okonomiyaki, make a smaller and thinner size so it is easier to flip.
9. Place the sliced pork belly on top of Okonomiyaki and cook covered for five minutes.
10. Gently press the okonomiyaki to fix the shape and keep it together. Cover and cook for another five minutes.
11. Flip over one last time and cook uncovered for two minutes. If you are going to cook next batch, transfer to a plate.
12. Serve with your preferred toppings.

4.7 Cheesy Ramen Carbonara

Cooking Time: 30 minutes

Serving Size: 4

Ingredients:
- Dashi, one cup
- Olive oil, one tbsp.

- Bacon slices, six
- Salt, as required
- Minced garlic, two
- Parsley, as required
- Parmesan cheese, half cup
- Milk, two tbsp.
- Eggs, two
- Ramen pack, three

Method:
1. Combine all the ingredients.
2. Boil noodles according to package instructions.
3. Save a quarter cup of cooking water to loosen sauce later, if needed. Drain noodles and toss with olive oil so that they do not stick.
4. Heat medium skillet over medium heat. Cook bacon pieces until brown and crisp. Add the noodles to the skillet and toss with the bacon until the noodles are coated in the bacon fat.
5. Beat eggs with fork and mix in parmesan cheese. Pour egg-cheese mixture to skillet and toss with bacon and noodles.
6. Divide between bowls. Garnish with parsley and freshly ground pepper.

4.8 Yakisoba

Cooking Time: 30 minutes

Serving Size: 4

Ingredients:

- Fish sauce, two tbsp.
- Egg, one
- Soy sauce, half cup
- Cooked Japanese rice, three cups
- Tomatoes, two
- Cilantro, half cup
- Salt and pepper, to taste
- Vegetable oil, two tbsp.
- Japanese chili peppers, three
- Toasted walnuts, half cup
- Chicken breast, eight ounces
- Onion, one
- Scallions, half cup
- Minced garlic, one tsp.

Instructions:

1. Heat a large nonstick pan over high heat.
2. Meanwhile, season chicken lightly with salt and pepper.
3. When the wok is very hot, add two tsp of the oil.
4. When the oil is hot, add the chicken and cook on high until it is browned all over and cooked through.
5. Remove chicken and set aside, add the eggs, pinch of salt and cook a minute or two until done.
6. Add the remaining oil to the wok and add the onion, scallions and garlic.

7. Sauté for a minute, add the chili pepper if using, tomatoes and stir in all the rice.
8. Add the soy sauce and fish sauce stir to mix all the ingredients.
9. Keep stirring a few minutes, and then add egg and chicken back to the wok.
10. Adjust soy sauce if needed and stir well for another 30 seconds.
11. Your dish is ready to be served.

4.9 Baked chicken Katsu

Cooking Time: 25 minutes

Serving Size: 4

Ingredients:
- Boneless chicken breast pieces, one pound
- Panko, one cup
- All-purpose flour, half cup
- Water, one tbsp.
- Egg, one
- Salt and pepper, to taste
- Tonkatsu sauce, as required

Instructions:
1. Gather all the ingredients. Adjust an oven rack to the middle position and preheat the oven to 400 degrees. Line a rimmed baking sheet with parchment paper.
2. Combine the panko and oil in a frying pan and toast over medium heat until golden brown. Transfer panko into a shallow dish and allow to cool down.

3. Butterfly the chicken breast and cut in half. Using a mallet or rolling pin, pound the chicken to equal thickness if necessary. Season salt and pepper on both sides of the chicken.

4. In a shallow dish, add flour and in another shallow dish, whisk together the egg and water.

5. Coat each chicken piece in the flour and shake off any excess flour. Dip into the egg mixture and then coat with the toasted panko, pressing firmly to adhere to the chicken.

6. Place the chicken pieces on the prepared baking sheet for about twenty minutes. Serve immediately or transfer to a wire rack so the bottom of the katsu does not get soggy from the moisture.

7. Serve with salad and tonkatsu sauce on the side.

4.10 Hayashi Ground Beef Curry

Cooking Time: 15 minutes

Serving Size: 2

Ingredients:

- Onion, one
- Carrots, half cup
- Ground beef, half pound
- Canola oil, one tbsp.
- Ketchup, two tbsp.
- Salt and pepper, to taste
- Corn starch, one tsp.
- Beef broth, one cup

- Sake, one tbsp.
- Boiled egg, one
- Worcestershire sauce, one tbsp.

Instructions:

1. Slice onion half. One half will be for frying; the other will go in with the dry curry.
2. Slice one half into thin half-moons. Finely chop the other one.
3. Boil egg and cut into small pieces or mash with a fork. Season well with salt and pepper.
4. Heat oil and add onions and carrots.
5. Sprinkle corn starch on top of ground beef and add to the vegetables. Add a quarter cup beef broth and break the ground beef while stirring.
6. Add beef broth, ketchup, sake, and Worcestershire sauce.
7. Mix well and cook for ten minutes or until all the liquid has evaporated. Season with salt and pepper.
8. Fry onions in a separate pan until crispy.
9. Put rice on a plate, top with curry, eggs and fried onions.

4.11 Ramen Noodle Skillet with Steak

Cooking Time: 15 minutes

Serving Size: 2

Ingredients:

- Onion, one
- Carrots, half cup

- Ground beef, half pound
- Canola oil, one tbsp.
- Ketchup, two tbsp.
- Salt and pepper, to taste
- Corn starch, one tsp.
- Beef broth, one cup
- Sake, one tbsp.
- Boiled egg, one
- Worcestershire sauce, one tbsp.

Instructions:

1. In a large skillet over medium-high heat, heat oil.
2. Add steak and sear until your desired completion, about five minutes per side for medium, then transfer to a cutting board and let it rest for five minutes, and then slice it.
3. In a small bowl, whisk together soy sauce, garlic, lime juice, honey, and cayenne until combined and set aside.
4. Add onion, peppers, and broccoli to skillet and cook until tender, then add soy sauce mixture and stir until fully coated.
5. Add cooked ramen noodles and steak and toss until combined.
6. Your dish is ready to be served.

4.12 Chicken Teriyaki

Cooking Time: 15 minutes

Serving Size: 2

Ingredients:

- Sesame oil, one tsp.
- Broccoli, for serving
- Honey, one tbsp.
- Ketchup, two tbsp.
- Salt and pepper, to taste
- Corn starch, one tsp.
- Cooked white rice, one cup
- Garlic and ginger, one tbsp.
- Boiled egg, one
- Soy sauce, one tbsp.

Instructions:

1. In a medium bowl, whisk together soy sauce, rice vinegar, oil, honey, garlic, ginger, and corn starch.
2. In a large skillet over medium heat, heat oil. Add chicken to skillet and season with salt and pepper. Cook until golden and almost cooked through.
3. Cover chicken and simmer until sauce is thickened slightly and chicken is cooked through.
4. Garnish with sesame seeds and green onions.
5. Serve over rice with steamed broccoli.

4.13 Japanese Salmon Bowl

Cooking Time: 30 minutes

Serving Size: 4

Ingredients:

- Chili sauce, one tsp.

- Soy sauce, one tsp.
- Rice, two cups
- Sesame oil, one tbsp.
- Ginger, two tbsp.
- Salt and pepper, to taste
- Sesame seeds, one tsp.
- Vinegar, one tsp.
- Shredded nori, as required
- Salmon, half pound
- Shredded cabbage, one cup

Instructions:

1. Place the rice, three cups of water and half teaspoon of salt in a large pot and bring to the boil.
2. Reduce the heat to low, place the lid on top and cook for fifteen minutes or until water is absorbed.
3. Remove from heat and let stand covered for five minutes.
4. Place the vinegar, soy sauce, chilli sauce, sesame oil, sesame seeds and ginger in a bowl and mix well.
5. Add the salmon and gently stir until completely coated.
6. Place the shredded cabbage and sesame oil in a bowl and mix until well combined.
7. Place a large spoonful of rice in each bowl, add the cabbage and squeeze over the mayonnaise.
8. Garnish with toasted shredded nori and toasted sesame seeds.

4.14 Scattered Sushi Rice/Chirashi-zushi

Cooking Time: 30 minutes

Serving Size: 4

Ingredients:

- Japanese rice, two cups
- Rice vinegar, a quarter cup
- Salt, one tsp.
- Sugar, two tbsp.
- Shitake mushrooms, eight
- Sashimi, half pound
- Eggs, three
- Mirin, one tsp.
- Sesame seeds, as required
- Tuna, half pound

Instructions:

1. Combine the ingredients.
2. Put rice in a large bowl and wash it with cold water. Repeat washing until the water becomes almost clear. Drain the rice in a colander and set aside for thirty minutes.
3. Place the rice in a rice cooker and add about two cups of water. Let the rice soak in the water for at least thirty minutes. Start the cooker.
4. In a small saucepan, mix rice vinegar, sugar, and salt. Put the pan on low heat and heat until the sugar dissolves. Cool the vinegar mixture.

5. Spread the hot steamed rice into a large plate or a large bowl. Sprinkle the vinegar mixture over the rice and quickly mix into the rice using a shamoji.
6. Meanwhile, remove stems from shiitake and slice thinly. Heat half cup of the reserved water used for rehydrating shiitake in a medium pan.
7. Add shiitake, soy sauce, sugar, and mirin. Simmer shiitake on low heat until the liquid is almost gone.
8. Make the omelettes by beating eggs in a bowl with sugar.
9. Oil a medium skillet and pour a scoop of egg mixture and make a thin omelette.
10. Serve sushi rice on a large plate or individual bowls.
11. Spread simmered shiitake, cucumber, imitation crab meat, and omelette strips over rice. Place tuna sashimi on top. Garnish with sesame seeds.

4.15 Broiled Shrimp and Vegetables/ Kushiyaki

Cooking Time: 10 minutes

Serving Size: 4

Ingredients:
- Lime juice, three tbsp.
- Shrimp, two pounds
- Salt and pepper, to taste
- Chili, one tbsp.
- Mix vegetables, one cup
- Sashimi, half pound
- Eggs, three

- Mirin, one tsp.
- Sesame seeds, as required

Instructions:

1. Marinate the shrimp with the spices, lime juice and olive oil.
2. Meanwhile, chop and slice the veggies.
3. Add one tablespoon of olive oil in a skillet and bring to medium heat.
4. Sauté the veggies until they obtain a golden colour and are tender. Remove and set aside in a bowl.
5. In the same skillet, sauté the shrimp until they are fully cooked. Then return the cookies veggies to the skillet, and sauté with the shrimps for two minutes.
6. Remove and serve.

4.16 Chicken in a Pot/Mizutaki

Cooking Time: 10 minutes

Serving Size: 4

Ingredients:

- Negi, one
- Mizuna, four
- Napa cabbage, eight
- Carrot, half cup
- Chicken thighs, one pound
- Kombu, half pound
- Sake, one tsp.
- Ginger, one tsp.

- Sesame seeds, as required

Instructions:

1. Mix all the ingredients.
2. In a large bowl, add five cups of water, and kombu to make cold brew kombu dashi. Set aside while you prepare the chicken.
3. Fill a medium pot with water and add the bone-in, skin-on chicken thigh pieces. Turn the heat on medium-low.
4. Bring the water to a boil and cook for one minute and discard the water.
5. Rinse the chicken, especially around the bone area, under lukewarm water.
6. In the cold brew kombu dashi, add the chicken thigh pieces you just rinsed.
7. Also add the chicken pieces sake, and ginger.
8. Bring it to a boil over medium heat.
9. Reduce the heat to medium-low and cook covered for thirty minutes. During this time, start preparing other ingredients. After thirty minutes, remove and discard the ginger slices.
10. Your dish is ready to be served.

Chapter 5: Japanese Salad Recipes

Regardless of the season, most Japanese meals are served with a salad to keep things in balance. A well-composed salad refreshes your palate, provides a pop of colour, and its crisp flavours enhance everything else on the table.

5.1 Japanese cucumber Salad (Sunomo)

Cooking Time: 10 minutes

Serving Size: 8

Ingredients:

- Peanuts, half cup
- Soy sauce, three tbsp.
- Sesame oil, one tsp.
- Sugar, one tbsp.
- Wine vinegar, three tbsp.
- Small cucumber, twelve ounces

- Garlic, one
- Fresh cilantro, as required

Instructions:

1. Whisk the dressing together and be sure to taste it to adjust anything you like.
2. Finely grind the peanuts in a food processor using the pulsing button. You want them to be very fine but be careful not to go too far and turn them into peanut butter.
3. Thinly slice the cucumbers in the diagonal shape.
4. If you would like to remove part of the peel first, you can run a zesting tool down the sides, or simply run the tines of a fork down the sides to create a decorative edge.
5. Put the cucumbers in a bowl and toss with enough dressing to coat thoroughly, you may not need all of it.
6. Toss with the crushed peanuts, sprinkle with chili flakes, and top with cilantro leaves.
7. Serve immediately or chill until ready to serve.

5.2 Japanese Watercess Salad

Cooking Time: 10 minutes

Serving Size: 2

Ingredients:

- Peanut butter, three tbsp.
- Rice vinegar, one tbsp.
- Honey, one tsp.
- Sugar, one tbsp.

- Wine vinegar, three tbsp.
- Watercress, six cups
- Mirin, two tbsp.

Instructions:

1. In a medium size pot, bring water, salted with one tablespoon kosher salt, to boil.
2. Put the peanut butter, honey, rice vinegar, soy sauce, and mirin in a medium bowl.
3. Rinse the watercress, drain and separate the leaves from the stems.
4. Roughly chop the stems and add to the boiling water along with the leaves.
5. Cook until the stems are tender but yielding a soft crunch.
6. Drain, rinse under cold water and softly squeeze out excess water.
7. Gently pat the watercress, dry with a paper towel and add to a mixing bowl.
8. Pour the dressing over the watercress and toss until the watercress is evenly coated.

5.3 Kani Salad

Cooking Time: 10 minutes

Serving Size: 4

Ingredients:

- Carrot, one medium
- Cucumber, two medium sized
- Ripe mango, one cup

- Japanese mayonnaise, one tbsp.
- Half lemon
- Salt and pepper to taste
- Kani, 150 g

Instructions:

1. Peel the carrots and trim off the ends.
2. Do the same with the cucumber but do not include the core with seeds.
3. Shred the crab sticks by hand by gently pressing a piece from end to end to loosen the strips and then separate each strip from one another.
4. Peel the ripe mango.
5. In a large bowl, add the cucumber, carrots, Kani, mango and Japanese mayo. Squeeze the juices of half a lemon on top and toss.
6. Season with salt and pepper as needed, and give it another toss until all ingredients are well blended.
7. Serve immediately or refrigerate until ready.
8. Serve on top of a layer of iceberg or romaine lettuce.

5.4 Oshitashi

Cooking Time: 5 minutes

Serving Size: 1

Ingredients:

- Spinach, one pound
- Sesame seeds, one tbsp.
- Soy sauce, one tbsp.

- Mirin, one tbsp.

Instructions:

1. Toast the sesame seeds in a skillet until lightly coloured.
2. Add the spinach to a large saucepan of boiling water and cook two to three minutes until wilted.
3. Have an ice bath ready.
4. Drain the spinach in a colander.
5. Squeeze dry and place in a bowl.
6. Mix the cooked spinach with the soy sauce, mirin and sesame seeds.
7. Serve at room temperature.

5.5 Japanese Cabbage Salad

Cooking Time: 5 minutes

Serving Size: 1

Ingredients:

- Coleslaw mix, one cup
- Sesame seeds, one tbsp.
- Soy sauce, one tbsp.
- Mirin, one tbsp.
- Bonito flakes, as required

Instructions:

1. Mix all the ingredients for the dressing together in a bowl and pour it over the shredded coleslaw mix.
2. Toss well and top with sesame seeds and bonito flakes.

5.6 Ramen Noodle Salad

Cooking Time: 15 minutes

Serving Size: 1

Ingredients:

- Cabbage and onion, one cup
- Sesame seeds, one tbsp.
- Soy sauce, one tbsp.
- Sugar, one tbsp.
- Vinegar, one tbsp.
- Butter, as required
- Ramen noodles, one pack
- Almonds, as required

Instructions:

1. Combine the oil, vinegar, sugar, and soy sauce in a jar and shake until the sugar is dissolved.
2. Melt the butter in a large skillet over medium heat. While the butter is melting, crush the ramen noodles while still inside the package.
3. Remove the seasoning packet and throw away.
4. Add the noodles, almonds, and sesame seeds to the melted butter in the skillet.
5. Sauté while stirring frequently, until the noodle mixture is golden brown.
6. Shred the cabbage and combine the cabbage and onions in a large mixing bowl. Add the noodle mixture.
7. Pour the dressing over the salad and toss well to combine.

8. Serve immediately.

5.7 Pork Chimichurri Salad

Cooking Time: 15 minutes

Serving Size: 2

Ingredients:

- Pork chops, one pound
- Greens, six ounces
- Cherry tomatoes, two cups
- Olive oil, one tbsp.
- Vinegar, one tbsp.
- Parsley, as required
- Chipotle, half
- Oregano leaves, as required
- Salt and pepper, as required
- Chimichurri dressing, per taste

Instructions:

1. In a food processor, combine olive oil, vinegar, parsley, oregano leaves, and chipotle. Season with salt and pepper and set aside.
2. Preheat a broiler. Line a rimmed baking sheet with foil and spray with cooking oil.
3. Place pork on the baking sheet and sprinkle both sides with salt and pepper. Broil until internal temperature reaches 145 degrees, five minutes per side. Remove pork from broiler and let it rest for five minutes.

4. Meanwhile, in a large bowl, combine greens, cherry tomatoes, cheese, and chimichurri dressing to taste. Arrange salad on plates or a platter.
5. Arrange on top of salad, drizzle with additional dressing, and serve.

5.8 Spring Green Salad

Cooking Time: 30 minutes

Serving Size: 4

Ingredients:
- Salad potatoes, half pound
- Petits pois, half cup
- Asparagus, half cup
- Olive oil, four tbsp.
- Pumpkin seeds, one tbsp.
- Spring onions, four
- Baby courgettes, one cup
- Whole grain mustard, as required
- Salt and pepper, as required
- Honey, per taste
- Lemon juice, as required

Instructions:
1. To make the dressing, put all the ingredients in a small food processor or blender and process until smooth and emulsified. Season well.

2. Cook the potatoes in lightly salted boiling water for ten minutes, or until just tender, adding the petits pois for the last two minutes.
3. Drain and place in a wide, shallow serving bowl.
4. Heat a large griddle pan or heavy-based frying pan until hot. Add a tablespoon of olive oil and add the asparagus in a single layer.
5. Cook for five minutes, or until lightly charred. Remove from the pan and add to the potato mixture.
6. Wipe out the pan and add the remaining olive oil. When hot, add the courgettes, sliced side down, and cook for five minutes, or until lightly charred. Add to the potato mixture with the lettuce and spring onions.
7. Stir the dressing then pour over the salad and mix well. Scatter over the pumpkin seeds and serve.

5.9 Japanese Corn Salad

Cooking Time: 30 minutes

Serving Size: 4

Ingredients:
- Mayonnaise, one tbsp.
- Cabbage, one
- Corn, half cup
- Sugar, one tbsp.
- Salt and pepper, as per taste
- Ground sesame seeds, two tbsp.

Instructions:

1. Shred the cabbage and drain the excess water. To allow a nice texture, do not shred it too thinly.
2. To prepare the dressing, mix the ingredients together.
3. In another bowl, mix the cabbage and corn. Add the dressing and you are done.
4. Add the dressing right before serving as the cabbage tends to get watery.
5. Your dish is ready to be served.

Chapter 6: Japanese Soup Recipes

The Japanese cuisine contains a variety of healthy and nutritious soups that are loved by many people all over the world. Following are the yummy and easy to make soup recipes that you can try on your own.

6.1 Miso soup

Cooking Time: 15 minutes

Serving Size: 4

Ingredients:

- Water, four cups
- Miso paste, three tbsp.
- Green onions, two
- Dashi granules, two tbsp.
- Tofu, one block

Instructions:
1. In a medium saucepan over medium-high heat, combine dashi granules and water; bring to a boil.
2. Reduce heat to medium, and whisk in the miso paste, and then stir in tofu.
3. Separate the layers of the green onions, and add them to the soup.
4. Simmer gently for a few minutes before serving.
5. Your soup is ready to be served.

6.2 Ochazuke

Cooking Time: 5 minutes

Serving Size: 1

Ingredients:
- Dashi, one tbsp.
- Soy sauce, one tsp.
- Japanese green tea leaves, one
- Water, one cup
- Salt and pepper to taste
- Mirin, one tsp.

Instructions:
1. Combine all the ingredients in a small saucepan and bring it to a boil.
2. Pour the soup into a small teapot.
3. Put tea leaves in the pot.
4. Bring the water to the appropriate temperature for your tea and pour it into the pot.

5. Set aside for two minutes.
6. Your soup is ready to be served.

6.3 Ozoni

Cooking Time: 20 minutes

Serving Size: 4

Ingredients:
- Dashi, one cup
- Soy sauce, one tbsp.
- Sake, one tbsp.
- Chicken strips, one pound
- Water, two cups
- Salt and pepper to taste

Instructions:
1. Mix all the ingredients together and let it simmer.
2. Your soup is ready to be served.

6.4 Japanese Clear Onions Soup

Cooking Time: one hour

Serving Size: 5

Ingredients:
- Vegetable oil, two tbsp.
- Onion, one
- Carrot, one cup
- Garlic and ginger paste, one tbsp.
- Chicken broth, one cup

- Beef broth, one cup
- Salt and pepper as required

Instructions:
1. Place a large stock pot over medium-high heat.
2. Add the oil and place the onion, garlic, carrots, and ginger in the pot.
3. Sear the veggies on all sides to caramelize, making sure not to burn the garlic.
4. Pour in the chicken broth, beef broth, and water.
5. Bring to a boil.
6. Lower the heat to a low boil and simmer for at least one hour.
7. Use a skimmer to remove the vegetables from the broth.
8. Taste, then adjust salt as needed.
9. Your dish is ready to be served.

6.5 Wonton Dumplings Soup

Preparation time: 12 minutes

Cooking Time: 30 minutes

Serving: 6

Ingredients:
- Wonton wrappers, twenty-four
- Finely chopped scallion, one tsp.
- Finely chopped ginger, one tsp.
- Soy sauce, one tbsp.
- Brown sugar, one tsp.

- Chicken breast, shredded, two
- Fresh spinach, one cup
- Shrimp, one pound
- Water chestnuts, eight ounces
- Mushroom, sliced, one cup
- Rice wine, one tbsp.
- Ground pork, eight ounces

Instructions:
1. Bring chicken stock to a rolling boil, and then add all the ingredients.
2. Cook until chicken and shrimps are cooked through, for about 10 minutes.
3. In a bowl, mix the pork, ground shrimp, brown sugar, rice wine or sherry, soy sauce, scallions and chopped ginger.
4. Blend well and set aside for 25-30 minutes for flavors to blend.
5. Add one tsp. of the filling in the center of each wonton wrapper.
6. Wet the edges of each wonton with a little water and press them together with your fingers to seal.
7. To cook, add wontons to the boiling chicken stock and cook for 4-5 minutes.
8. Transfer to individual soup bowls and serve.

6.6 Kimchi and Tofu Soup

Cooking Time: 20 minutes

Serving Size: 2

Ingredients:

- Vegetable oil, one tbsp.
- Scallions, six
- Kimchi, half cup
- Chicken broth, one cup
- Soy sauce, three tbsp.
- Salt and pepper, as per taste
- Garlic and ginger paste, one tbsp.
- Tofu, one block
- Daikon, one

Instructions:

1. Heat oil in a large saucepan over high.
2. Cook white and pale-green parts of scallions, garlic, and ginger, stirring often, until softened and fragrant, about three minutes.
3. Add broth, then whisk in the soy sauce.
4. Add daikon and gently simmer until daikon is tender, fifteen minutes.
5. Add kimchi and tofu.
6. Simmer until tofu is heated through.
7. Carefully divide among bowls.
8. Your soup is ready to be served.

6.7 Shio Koji Mushroom Soup

Cooking Time: 20 minutes

Serving Size: 2

Ingredients:

- Soup stock, two cups
- Different mushrooms, two cups
- Salt and pepper to taste
- Shio koji, two tbsp.

Instructions:

1. Slice the mushrooms into thin slices or pieces and boil in plenty of water for about two mins.
2. Drain and add the shio koji seasoning to the hot mushrooms.
3. Wait about fifteen minutes for the flavours to develop.
4. In another saucepan, bring soup stock to the boil.
5. Add the mushrooms and salt and allow everything to heat through.
6. Spoon into bowls and serve with some nice crusty bread.

6.8 Yudofu

Cooking Time: 15 minutes

Serving Size: 2

Ingredients:

- Tofu, one block
- Mitsuba, as required
- Sake, one tbsp.
- Mirin, one tsp.
- Vegetable stock, three cups
- Water, one cup

Instructions:

1. Mix all the ingredients well and let it simmer for fifteen minutes.
2. Your soup is ready to be served.

6.9 Ojiya Rice Soup

Cooking Time: 20 minutes

Serving Size: 2

Ingredients:

- Japanese rice, one cup
- Vegetable stock, two cups
- Mixed vegetable, one cup
- Soy sauce, one tsp.
- Mirin, half tsp.
- Salt and pepper, to taste
- Water, two cups

Instructions:

1. Mix all the ingredients well and let it simmer for fifteen minutes.
2. Your soup is ready to be served.

6.10 Oshiruko Sweet Red Bean Soup

Cooking Time: 20 minutes

Serving Size: 3

Ingredients:

- Azuki sweet red beans, one cup

- Mochi rice cakes, four
- Vegetable stock, four cups

Instructions:
1. Start by adding the azuki and one cup for water to a large pan and bring it to the boil. You can adjust the amount of water depending if you prefer a thick or thin soup.
2. You can cook the mochi in a variety of ways, but grilling them gives great results so place the mochi under a hot grill for five to ten minutes.
3. Once the mochi begin expanding in the grill, they are ready and can be put into serving bowls.
4. After the azuki and water mix is boiled, take it off the heat and pour over the mochi in the serving bowls and enjoy.

6.11 Bean Paste Soup

Cooking Time: 15 minutes

Serving Size: 2

Ingredients:
- Bean paste, five tbsp.
- Vegetable soup, two cups
- Soy sauce, one tsp.
- Mirin, one tsp.
- Salt and pepper to taste

Instructions:
1. Mix all the ingredients well and let it simmer for fifteen minutes.

2. Your soup is ready to be served.

6.12 Egg Drop Soup

Cooking Time: 30 minutes

Serving: 6

Ingredients:

- Cornstarch, two tbsp.
- Eggs, two
- Green Onions, chopped, three
- Ginger, grated, half tsp.
- Water, two tbsp.
- Chicken broth, four cups
- Soy Sauce, one tbsp.

Instructions:

1. Mix all the ingredients together, and boil it for about thirty minutes.
2. Add the cornstarch in the end, and mix properly.
3. Your soup is ready to be served.

Chapter 7: Japanese Snacks

Japanese snacks are appreciated worldwide for the variety of snacks. The tastes are unique and also healthy. Following are some amazing snack recipes that you can try at home.

7.1 Japanese Summer Sandwiches

Cooking Time: 5 minutes

Serving: 2

Ingredients:
- Bread slices, six
- Strawberry, one cup
- Whipped cream, one cup

Instructions:

1. First you should prepare your bread.
2. Either whip half cup of whipping cream in a bowl until stiff and spread evenly on the bread.
3. Next, wash, cut off the stems and chop each strawberry in half down the middle.
4. Your sandwich is ready to be served.

7.2 Fresh Spring Rolls with Japanese Style Sauce

Cooking Time: 20 minutes

Serving: 4

Ingredients:

- Prawns, half pound
- Green beans, one cup
- Mint or coriander leaves, as required
- Rice paper wrapper, twelve
- Spring onion, half cup
- Mayonnaise, two tbsp.
- Bean chili paste, one tsp.
- Miso paste, one tsp.

Instructions:

1. Fill a small saucepan with some water and add a little salt.
2. Add the prawns and boil until they are bright pink for about five mins.
3. In a separate saucepan, boil the green beans for five mins.

4. Lay the rice paper on clean cloth.
5. Arrange the mint or coriander leaves on the bottom of the rice paper and add the prawn halves in the middle.
6. Top with the green beans and one whole chives or spring onion.
7. Sprinkle a little salt on top to taste.
8. Fold the sides in and tightly roll to ensure all ingredients are inside.
9. Make the dipping sauce by mixing all the ingredients together.
10. Serve spring rolls with the dipping sauce as a snack or side.

7.3 Karaage Japanese Fried Chicken

Cooking Time: 30 minutes

Serving: 6

Ingredients:

- Soy sauce, three tbsp.
- Boneless Chicken thighs, one pound
- Sake, one tbsp.
- Gaelic and ginger paste, one tsp.
- Katakuriko potato starch, a quarter cup
- Japanese mayonnaise, as required
- Cooking oil, as required

Instructions:

1. Cut chicken into bite-size pieces.

2. Add the ginger, garlic, soy sauce and cooking sake to a bowl and mix until combined.
3. Add the chicken, coat well, and allow marinating for twenty minutes.
4. Drain any excess liquid from the chicken and add your katakuriko potato starch. Mix until the pieces are fully coated.
5. Heat some cooking oil in a pan to around 180 degrees and test the temperature by dropping in some flour.
6. Fry a few pieces at a time for a few minutes until they are deep golden-brown colour, then remove and allow to drain on a wire rack or kitchen roll.
7. Serve hot or cold with some lemon wedges and a squeeze of Japanese mayonnaise.

7.4 Tazukuri Candied Sardines

Cooking Time: 15 minutes

Serving: 4

Ingredients:

- Toasted sesame seeds, one tbsp.
- Honey, one tbsp.
- Soy sauce, one tbsp.
- Sugar, one tbsp.
- Honey, one tbsp.
- Flavored oi, one tbsp.
- Sake, one tsp.
- Baby sardines, one cup

Instructions:

1. Gather all the ingredients. You will also need a baking sheet lined with parchment paper.
2. Put dried baby sardines in a frying pan, and toast them on medium-low heat for a few minutes or until crispy.
3. Add the sesame seeds in the frying pan and toast for two minutes.
4. Make sure to shake the pan constantly so the sesame seeds do not burn.
5. In the same frying pan, add sake, soy sauce, and sugar.
6. Add honey and oil.
7. Bring to a simmer on medium-low heat and reduce the sauce until the sauce gets thicken and you can draw a line on the surface of the pan with a silicone spatula.
8. Add the sardines back to the pan and coat with the sauce.
9. Once the sardines are coated with the sauce nicely, transfer back to the parchment paper.
10. Your dish is ready to be served.

7.5 Kuromame Sweetened Black Soybean

Cooking Time: 4 hours

Serving: 8

Ingredients:

- Water, five cups
- Sugar, two tbsp.
- Soy sauce, one tbsp.

- Edible gold leaf flakes, as required
- Black soybeans, one cup
- Kosher salt, as required

Instructions:
1. Gather all the ingredients.
2. Rinse black soybeans under running water and discard bad ones.
3. Put black soybeans and water in a large pot and let it soak overnight.
4. After being soaked, add sugar and salt and gently mix.
5. Start cooking over medium heat. Once boiling, you start to see white bubbles. When it is done, put an Otoshibuta and a regular pot lid.
6. The otoshibuta is to keep the soybeans under the cooking liquid.
7. Reduce heat to low and simmer for four hours or until the beans are tender.
8. Check inside the pot a few times to make sure there is enough cooking liquid.
9. Check if the beans are tender by mashing a bean with two fingers.
10. When the means are tender, add soy sauce and mix well.
11. Remove from the heat and place the parchment paper on top of the surface to prevent the beans from getting wrinkles.
12. Once cooled, keep in the refrigerator overnight so the soybeans will turn darker and absorb more flavour.

13. Your dish is ready to be served.

7.6 Takoyaki Octopus Balls

Cooking Time: 30 minutes
Serving: 6

Ingredients:
- Dashi stock powder, one tbsp.
- Eggs, two
- Flour, half cup
- Chopped boiled octopus, half cup
- Chopped spring onion, half cup
- Water, as required
- Tempura flakes, half tsp.
- Red picked ginger, half tsp.

Instructions:
1. Grab a large bowl and mix together eggs, flour, water and a little dashi stock.
2. Place your takoyaki plate on the gas stove on medium heat and heat up a small amount of oil in each hole.
3. Cut up your octopus into small pieces.
4. Place a piece of octopus in each of the semi-circular holes, and then fill up each hole to the top with the batter mix.

5. Now you can add the chopped spring onion, red pickled ginger and tempura flakes to each hole.
6. Once the takoyaki are about half cooked, you will need to flip them over.
7. Usually, you can only flip each takoyaki about three quarters of the way round so allow it to cook a little more before flipping it again.
8. Place a few takoyaki on a plate and smother them with loads of takoyaki sauce and Japanese mayonnaise.
9. Your dish is ready to be served.

7.7 Yakitori Grilled Skewers

Cooking Time: 10 minutes

Serving: 12

Ingredients:

- Teriyaki sauce, half cup
- Green shallots, two
- Chicken thigh, two pounds

Instructions:

1. Heat teriyaki sauce in a small saucepan medium-high heat. Bring to simmer and reduce to thicken the sauce.
2. Cut the white end part of the shallots into long pieces.
3. Prepare the skewers.
4. Preheat the BBQ grill and coat with olive oil.
5. Place the yakitori chicken skewers on the grill side to cook the chicken till browned.

6. Turn the skewers over and cook till other side browned or chicken meat change whitish colour.
7. Brush the Teriyaki sauce over the chicken skewers. When one side is coated, turn the skewers over and Brush Yakitori sauce over the side.
8. Repeat the above process one more time then turn the heat off.
9. Serve the yakitori skewers on rice or serve with green salad.

7.8 Sweet Ginger Meatballs

Cooking Time: 30 minutes

Serving: 4

Ingredients:

- Ginger and garlic paste, one tbsp.
- Eggs, one
- Ground turkey, one pound
- Sesame oil, half tsp.
- Soy sauce, four tbsp.
- Bread crumbs, half cup
- Hoisin, two tbsp.
- Diced scallions, as required
- Sesame seeds, as required

Instructions:

1. Pre-heat oven to 400 degrees and lightly grease a large baking sheet.

2. In a large bowl, add turkey, garlic, ginger, and mix well.
3. Then add egg, panko, sesame oil, and soy sauce, and mix well.
4. Roll out the meatballs and place on baking sheet.
5. Bake for ten mins and then rotate pan and bake for another ten minutes.
6. Heat a large sauté pan to medium.
7. Transfer meatballs to a large sauté pan that will fit them all.
8. In a small bowl mix the remaining soy sauce and hoisin.
9. Coat and turn meatballs in sauce as it bubbles and thickens and let cook for a couple of minutes.
10. Remove meatballs, add to a bowl and pour remaining sauce on meatballs.
11. Serve as an appetizer or over a layer of rice.

7.9 Satsuma Age Fried Fish Cake with Vegetables

Cooking Time: 30 minutes

Serving: 4

Ingredients:
- Sugar, two tbsp.
- Eggs, one
- Fish fillet, one pound
- Salt, as required
- Ginger juice, half tsp.

- Water, two tbsp.
- Mix vegetables, two cups
- Soy Sauce, one tbsp.

Instructions:
1. Cut fish fillet into small pieces so that it is easier to make paste in a food processor.
2. Add fish pieces, sake, ginger juice, salt and sugar to a food processor and whizz until the mixture becomes paste.
3. Add egg to the fish paste and blend well.
4. Add all the vegetable mixture in a large bowl and mix well ensuring that vegetable pieces are evenly coated with corn flour.
5. This will allow the vegetables to stick to the paste better.
6. Add the fish paste to the bowl and mix well.
7. Heat oil in a deep-frying pan or a skillet to 170 degrees.
8. Take the fish cake mixture and make a ball.
9. Fry until bottom side of the fish cake is golden brown.
10. Turn it over to cook until golden brown.
11. Remove the fish cake and drain oil on a rack or kitchen paper.
12. Serve while hot or at room temperature with lemon wedges, or grated ginger.

7.10 Sweet and Salty Nori Seaweed Popcorn

Cooking Time: 30 minutes

Serving: 6

Ingredients:

- Black sesame seeds, one tbsp.
- Brown sugar, one tbsp.
- Salt, half tsp.
- Coconut oil, half tsp.
- Popcorn kernel, half cup
- Butter, two tbsp.
- Nori seaweed flakes, one tbsp.

Instructions:

1. In a pestle and mortar, grind the nori seaweed flakes, sesame seeds, sugar and salt to a fine powder.
2. Melt the coconut oil in a large, heavy-bottomed saucepan.
3. Add popcorn kernels, cover with a lid and cook over a medium heat until they pop.
4. Immediately add the rest of the corn after the corn is popped, replace the lid and cook, shaking the pan occasionally until all the kernels are popped.
5. Transfer the popped corn to a large bowl and pour over the melted butter, if using.
6. Sprinkle over your sweet and salty nori mixture and use your hands to mix well until every piece is coated.
7. Top with the remaining sesame seeds.

Chapter 8: Japanese Desserts

Japanese cuisine is famous for its amazing dessert ranges. Here in this section where we will discuss the yummiest dessert recipes of Japan.

8.1 Kinako Dango

Cooking Time: 5 minutes

Serving: 4

Ingredients:
- Kinako, half cup
- Granulated sugar, two tbsp.
- Cold water, half cup
- Dango powder, one cup
- Kosher salt, half tsp.

Instructions:

1. In a mixing bowl add Dango powder and water. Mix well until well combined.
2. Grab a little dough and shape into a ball.
3. Lay it on a plate and repeat until all the dough is used.
4. Set aside a bowl of cold water.
5. Add dango balls to boiling water and boil until they rise to the top.
6. Drain and add to cold water. Leave for a few minutes until they cool down and drain.
7. In another mixing bowl, add kinako, sugar and salt, and mix well.
8. Put a half of the kinako mixture in a serving bowl, add dango balls, and top with leftover kinako.
9. Your meal is ready to be served.

8.2 Japanese Style Pumpkin Pudding

Cooking Time: 25 minutes

Serving: 2

Ingredients:

- Pumpkin puree, one cup
- Sugar, three tbsp.
- Vanilla extract, one tsp.
- Eggs, two
- Gelatin powder, two tbsp.
- Maple syrup, as required

Instructions:
1. Dissolve the gelatin powder with the milk.
2. Meanwhile, put the pumpkin puree and sugar in a bowl, stir, and microwave on high for thirty seconds.
3. Stir in the milk and gelatin mix and add it to the pumpkin and sugar. Stir in the eggs and vanilla extract and combine well.
4. Get rid of the unblended bits left in the strainer.
5. Place a deep pan or pot over a burner and put the ramekins inside.
6. Turn the heat on and bring the water to a boil.
7. Turn the heat off and check the firmness of the puddings. The texture should be a little firm but still creamy like pudding.
8. Cool the puddings in the fridge until they are completely chilled.
9. Pour two tablespoons of pure maple syrup on top of each pudding before serving.

8.3 Dorayaki

Cooking Time: 15 minutes

Serving: 6

Ingredients:
- Honey, two tbsp.
- Eggs, two
- Sugar, one cup
- Flour, one cup
- Baking powder, one tsp.

- Red bean paste, half cup

Instructions:

1. Gather all the ingredients.
2. In a large bowl, combine eggs, sugar, and honey and whisk well until the mixture becomes fluffy.
3. Sift flour and baking powder into the bowl and mix all together.
4. The batter should be slightly smoother now.
5. Heat a large non-stick frying pan over medium-low heat. It is best to take your time and heat slowly.
6. When you see the surface of the batter starting to bubble, flip over and cook the other side.
7. Put the red bean paste in the centre.
8. Wrap dorayaki with plastic wrap until ready to be served.

8.4 Fluffy Japanese Cheesecake

Cooking Time: 50 minutes

Serving: 4-5

Ingredients:

- Vanilla ice cream
- Brownie mix, one box
- Hot fudge sauce

Instructions:

1. Preheat oven to 350 degrees.
2. Cut strips of foil to line jumbo muffin tin cups.

3. Layer strips in crisscross manner to use as lifting handles when brownies are done.
4. Spray foil in a pan with cooking spray.
5. Prepare brownie batter as described on the back of the box or according to your favorite recipe.
6. Divide batter evenly among muffin tin cups. Muffin cups will be about 3/4 full.
7. Place muffin tin on the rimmed baking sheet and bake in preheated oven for 40-50 minutes.
8. Remove from oven and cool in the pan for 5 minutes, then transfer to a cooling rack for ten additional minutes.
9. You may need to use a butter knife or icing spatula to loosen the sides of each brownie and then lift out of the muffin pan using the foil handles.
10. Serve warm brownie on a plate topped with a scoop of vanilla ice cream and hot fudge sauce.

8.5 Matcha Ice cream

Cooking Time: 5 minutes

Serving: 2

Ingredients:

- Matcha powder, three tbsp.
- Half and half, two cups
- Kosher salt, a pinch
- Sugar, half cup

Instructions:

1. In a medium saucepan, whisk together the half and half, sugar, and salt.
2. Start cooking the mixture over medium heat, and add green tea powder.
3. Remove from the heat and transfer the mixture to a bowl sitting in an ice bath. When the mixture is cool, cover with plastic wrap and chill in the refrigerator.
4. Your dish is ready to be served.

8.6 Taiyaki

Cooking Time: 15 minutes

Serving: 5

Ingredients:

- Cake flour, two cups
- Baking powder, one tsp.
- Baking soda, half tsp.
- Sugar, one cup
- Egg, two
- Milk, half cup

Instructions:

1. Sift the cake flour, baking powder and baking soda into a large bowl.
2. Add the sugar and whisk well to combine.
3. In a medium bowl, whisk the egg and then add the milk.
4. Combine the dry ingredients with wet ingredients and whisk well.
5. Pour the batter into a measuring cup or jug.

6. Heat the Taiyaki pan and grease the pan with vegetable oil using a brush.
7. Fill the Taiyaki pan mould about 60% full over medium-low heat.
8. Close the lid and immediately turn.
9. Then flip and cook. Open and check to see if Taiyaki is golden coloured.
10. Let Taiyaki cool on a wire rack.
11. Your dish is ready to be served.

8.7 Zenzai

Cooking Time: 15 minutes

Serving: 4

Ingredients:

- Mochi, one cup
- Red beans, one cup
- Sugar, three tbsp.

Instructions:

1. Place red beans, and five cups of water in a pot.
2. Bring to a boil and cook for five minutes, and then, strain the beans and discard the water they were cooked in.
3. Now, drain the beans, reserving the water they were cooked in.
4. Put drained beans into the pot, add sugar, and cook over medium heat for ten minutes, stirring constantly.
5. Then, pour in the water from cooking the beans, season with sugar, and stir over low heat.

6. Bake mochi over a grill or in a toaster oven until they expand and brown slightly.
7. Put mochi into a serving bowl and cover with a scoop of bean soup.
8. Your dish is ready to be served.

8.8 Okoshi

Cooking Time: 10 minutes

Serving: 3

Ingredients:

- Cooked rice, one cup
- Tempura oil, one tbsp.
- Sugar, one cup
- Puffed rice, one cup
- Peanuts, half cup

Instructions:

1. Spread the cooked rice on a baking sheet in a thin layer and place it on a flat sieve or a serving tray.
2. When the rice becomes translucent and crispy, it is ready for further preparation. First, break down any lumps using your fingers.
3. Line a mould for okoshi with baking paper.
4. Heat tempura oil to 180 degrees and deep fry the rice.
5. Mix sugar with water and cook over medium heat until the syrup starts simmering, then lower the heat and, if you wish, add peanuts.

6. Combine fried, puffed rice and sugar syrup quickly, and transfer to a container. Cover the top with a baking sheet, and press with a heavy and flat object.
7. Cut into small pieces and serve.

8.9 Dango

Cooking Time: 10 minutes

Serving: 6

Ingredients:

- Joshinko rice flour, one cup
- Shiratamako rice flour, one cup
- Sugar, half cup
- Hot water, as required

Instructions:

1. Mix together the joshinko non-glutinous rice flour, shiratamako glutinous rice flour and sugar.
2. Add the hot water little by little, mixing well.
3. Cover the bowl you mixed your dango mixture in and microwave for a few minutes. Dampen your hands again and roll the dough into evenly sized balls.
4. Your dish is ready to be served.

8.10 Kasutera

Cooking Time: 50 minutes

Serving: 24

Ingredients:

- Milk, one cup

- Honey, two tbsp.
- Flour, two cups
- Sugar, one cup

Instructions:
1. Set the oven to preheat to 170 degrees.
2. First, coat the bottom and the sides of a baking pan with butter or shortening, and then line it with baking paper, so that a portion of the paper is hanging over the sides of the pan.
3. Sprinkle the bottom of the pan with sugar.
4. Bring a pot of water to a boil, and then remove from the heat.
5. Whisk milk and honey together and double sift the flour.
6. Add the eggs and the sugar to the bowl.
7. Next, whisk in the milk and honey mixture, and then add flour tablespoon by tablespoon, whisking all the time until incorporated.
8. When the cake is cool enough to handle, put the cake into a plastic bag and seal. Refrigerate for a few hours.
9. Your dish is ready to be served.

8.11 Daifuku

Cooking Time: 10 minutes

Serving: 6

Ingredients:
- Swedish dried peas, two tbsp.

- Caster sugar, two tbsp.
- Rice flour, two cups
- Potato starch, one cup
- Anko red bean paste, two tbsp.

Instructions:
1. Place the Swedish red peas in a small saucepan and pour enough water to cover the red peas.
2. Bring it to simmer over low heat and cook for ten minutes.
3. Divide the anko sweet red bean paste into six balls.
4. Place the Shiratamako in a mixing bowl and add sugar and water.
5. Cover your hand with katakuriko potato starch and spread the mochi dough out with your hand.
6. Place the Swedish red peas over the mochi dough and fold the mochi dough in half.
7. Take one piece of dough on your palm and flat it.
8. Close the mochi ends at the top with your well dusted finger and shape it into a nice round shaped daifuku mochi.

Chapter 9: Ramen and Sushi Recipes

Japanese ramen and sushi are famous worldwide. They are appreciated by many individuals all around the globe. Following are some recipes you can make at home:

9.1 Shoyu Ramen

Cooking Time: 30 minutes

Serving: 4

Ingredients:

- Chashu, one cup
- Nitamago, as required
- Shiitake, as required
- La-yu, as required
- Nori, half cup
- Ramen, four packs
- Dashi, half cup

Instructions:

1. In a pot of salted boiling water, cook ramen, stirring with tongs or chopsticks until cooked, about one minute.
2. In a small saucepan over medium heat, warm dashi and shiitake until barely simmering.
3. Cook for one minute and remove from heat.
4. Set shiitake aside.
5. Add dashi and noodles to serving bowl.
6. Top with chashu, nitamago, shiitake, green onion, a drizzle of la-yu, and nori, if desired.

9.2 Miso Ramen

Cooking Time: 10 minutes

Serving: 2

Ingredients:

- Miso paste, two tbsp.
- Mix vegetables, one cup
- Ramen, two packs
- Soy sauce, one tbsp.

Instructions:

1. Cook the ramen, and boil the vegetables.
2. Now mix all the remaining ingredients, and serve hot.

9.3 Simple Homemade Chicken Ramen

Cooking Time: 10 minutes

Serving: 2

Ingredients:
- Chicken, one cup
- Ramen noodles, two packs
- Oil, one tsp.
- Salt and pepper to taste

Instructions:
1. Cook the ramen, and chicken.
2. Now mix all the other ingredients, and serve hot.

9.4 Vegetarian Ramen

Cooking Time: 10 minutes

Serving: 2

Ingredients:
- Mix vegetables, one cup
- Ramen noodles, two packs
- Oil, one tsp.
- Salt and pepper to taste

Instructions:
1. Cook the ramen, and vegetables.
2. Now mix all the other ingredients, and serve hot.

9.5 Ramen Noodles

Cooking Time: 10 minutes

Serving: 2

Ingredients:

- Ramen noodles, two packs
- Miso paste, two tbsp.
- Soy Sauce, one tbsp.

Instructions:

1. Mix all the ingredients together, and cook well for ten minutes.
2. Your dish is ready to be served

9.6 Pork Ramen

Cooking Time: 10 minutes

Serving: 2

Ingredients:

- Pork meat, one cup
- Ramen noodles, two packs
- Oil, one tsp.
- Salt and pepper to taste

Instructions:

1. Cook the ramen, and pork meat.
2. Now mix all the ingredients, and serve hot.

9.7 Instant Ramen

Cooking Time: 10 minutes

Serving: 2

Ingredients:

- Instant ramen noodles, two packs
- Instant spice mix, two tbsp.
- Water, three cups

Instructions:

1. Mix all the ingredients together and cook for ten minutes.
2. Your dish is ready to be served.

9.8 Sushi

Cooking Time: 5 minutes

Serving: 4

Ingredients:

- Sesame oil, half tsp.
- Green onions/scallions, two
- Toasted white sesame seeds, two tbsp.
- Spicy Mayo, two tbsp.
- Sushi rice (cooked and seasoned), one and a half cup
- Sashimi-grade tuna, four ounces
- Sriracha sauce, three tsp.

Instructions:

1. In a medium bowl, combine the tuna, Sriracha sauce, sesame oil, and some of the green onion.
2. Lay a sheet of nori, shiny side down, on the bamboo mat. Wet your fingers in water and spread ¾ cup of the rice evenly onto nori sheet.
3. Sprinkle the rice with sesame seeds.
4. Turn the sheet of nori over so that the rice side is facing down.
5. Line the edge of nori sheet at the bottom end of the bamboo mat.
6. Place half of the tuna mixture at the bottom end of the nori sheet.
7. Grab the bottom edge of the bamboo mat while keeping the fillings in place with your fingers, roll into a tight cylinder form.
8. With a very sharp knife, cut the roll in half and then cut each half into three pieces.
9. Put a dollop of spicy mayo on top of each sushi and garnish with the remaining green onion.
10. Your dish is ready to be served.

9.9 Japanese Sushi Rolls

Cooking Time: 60 minutes

Serving: 4

Ingredients:
- Lemon, half
- Nori sheets, two
- Sushi rice, two cups

- Shrimp tempura, eight pieces
- Tobiko, two tbsp.
- Unagi (eel)
- Persian/Japanese cucumbers, one
- Avocados, one

Instructions:
1. Gather all the ingredients.
2. Cut cucumber lengthwise into quarters.
3. Remove the seeds, and then cut in half lengthwise.
4. Cut the avocado in half lengthwise around the seed, and twist the two halves until they are separate.
5. Hack the knife edge into the pit. Hold the skin of the avocado with the other hand, and twist in counter directions.
6. Remove the skin, and slice the avocado widthwise.
7. Gently press the avocado slices with your fingers, and then keep pressing gently, and evenly with the side of the knife until the length of avocado is about the length of sushi roll.
8. Wrap the bamboo mat with plastic wrap, and place half of the nori sheet, shiny side down.
9. Turn it over and put the shrimp tempura, cucumber strips, and tobiko at the bottom end of the nori sheet.
10. If you like to put unagi, place it inside here as well.
11. From the bottom end, start rolling nori sheet over the filling tightly, and firmly with bamboo mat until the bottom end reaches the nori sheet.

12. Place the bamboo mat over the roll and tightly squeeze the roll.
13. Using the side of the knife, place the avocado on top of the roll.
14. Place plastic wrap over the roll and then put the bamboo mat over.
15. Cut the roll into 8 pieces with the knife.
16. Put tobiko on each piece of sushi, and drizzle spicy mayo, and sprinkle black sesame seeds on top.
17. Your dish is ready to be served.

Chapter 10: Most Popular and Alternative Japanese Recipes

Japanese cuisine remains rooted in its traditions, while embracing a certain amount of fusion from other cultures. Following are some traditional and alternative recipes:

10.1 Sashimi

Cooking Time: 20-30 seconds

Serving: 3

Ingredients:

- Tuna, one pound
- Salmon, one pound, sesame oil, two tbsp.
- Coriander leaves, as required

Instructions:

1. Drizzle the tuna and salmon with sesame seed oil, turning it over to ensure even coverage on all sides.
2. Sprinkle a generous helping of dried and chopped coriander leaves over the tuna, and salmon filet.

3. Cook the fish for only fifteen to twenty seconds.
4. Your dish is ready to be served with your preferred sauce.

10.2 Unadon

Cooking Time: 20-30 seconds

Serving: 3

Ingredients:
- Sesame oil, two tbsp.
- Unagi eel, two pounds
- Japanese pepper one tbsp.
- Coriander leaves, one tbsp.

Instructions:
1. Drizzle the unagi with sesame seed oil, turning it over to ensure even coverage on all sides.
2. Sprinkle a generous amount of Japanese pepper, and chopped coriander leaves over the unagi.
3. Cook the fish for only fifteen to twenty seconds.
4. Your dish is ready to be served.

10.3 Tempura

Cooking Time: 10 minutes

Serving: 2

Ingredients:
- Plain flour, four tbsp.
- Prawns, one pound
- Mix vegetables, one cup

- Mayonnaise, half tsp.
- Water, two tbsp.

Instructions:

1. Prepare the prawn and vegetables and set aside.
2. Place the flour, and add icy cold water and mayonnaise.
3. Set aside in fridge until all ingredients and oil are ready.
4. Fill a deep pan or deep-fryer with vegetable oil and heat until 180 degrees.
5. Add each ingredient to the batter individually to coat them and put them into the oil.
6. Fry each ingredient.
7. Your dish is ready to be served with your preferred sauce

10.4 Soba

Cooking Time: 10 minutes

Serving: 2

Ingredients:

- Japanese noodles, one pack
- Sesame seeds, as required
- Sesame oil, one tbsp.
- Green Onions, chopped, three
- Ginger, grated, half tsp.
- Soy Sauce, one tbsp.

Instructions:
1. Boil the noodles properly and then mix all the ingredients together while on heat.
2. Your dish is ready to be served.

10.5 Udon

Cooking Time: 15 minutes

Serving: 2

Ingredients:
- Cornstarch, two tbsp.
- Japanese noodles, one pack
- Green Onions, chopped, three
- Ginger, grated, half tsp.
- Water, two tbsp.
- Chicken broth, four cups
- Soy Sauce, one tbsp.

Instructions:
1. Mix all the ingredients together and let it cook for fifteen minutes.
2. Now add the corn flour mixed in water.
3. Cook for five minutes.
4. Your dish is ready to be served.

10.6 Sukiyaki

Cooking Time: 30 minutes

Serving: 6

Ingredients:

- Dried vermicelli, two cups
- Tofu slices, six
- Shiitake mushrooms, half cup
- Enoki mushrooms, half cup
- Napa cabbage, one cup
- Tong ho, half cup
- Scallions, one cup
- Vegetable oil, two tbsp.
- Beef slices, six slices

Instructions:

1. Prepare all your sukiyaki ingredients, the tofu slices, rehydrated shiitake mushrooms, enoki mushrooms, napa cabbage, tong ho, and scallions.
2. Soak the dried vermicelli noodles in water for ten minutes.
3. Heat a tablespoon vegetable oil in the pan.
4. Fry the white parts of the scallions in the oil for two minutes.
5. In the pan with the scallions, add the sliced beef.
6. Sear the beef for a few seconds, and add a drizzle of your sukiyaki sauce.
7. Add the rest of your sukiyaki sauce and two cups stock.
8. Bring to a boil, and add the tofu, mushrooms, napa cabbage, and tong ho to the pot in sections.
9. Also drain the vermicelli noodles you soaked and add them to the pot.

10. Remove the cover, and add the beef back to the pot.
11. Sprinkle with the chopped scallions, and enjoy with rice and egg yolk.

10.7 Oden

Cooking Time: 30 minutes

Serving: 6

Ingredients:
- Dashi, three cups
- Fish cakes, six
- Fish balls, six
- Eggs, six
- Konnyaku, two
- Kombu, two
- Japanese mustard, two tbsp.
- Soy sauce, two tsp.
- Mirin, two tsp.
- Sake, two tsp.
- Togarashi, as required

Instructions:
1. Rinse the fish cakes and fish balls with running water, remove the excess oil from the fish cakes and fish balls.
2. In a soup pot, bring the dashi, water, kombu strips to boil.
3. Add the daikon and stew on low heat until they are cooked through.
4. Add the hard-boiled eggs, konnyaku, and fish cakes.

5. Add the soy sauce, mirin and sake. Turn the heat to low and simmer for fifteen minutes.
6. Serve the Oden warm with Japanese mustard and Togarashi.

10.8 Gohan - Steamed Rice

Cooking Time: 10 minutes

Serving: 2

Ingredients:
- Japanese rice, one cup
- Water, one and a half cup
- Salt for taste

Instructions:
1. Wash the rice and then cook it properly.
2. Pour water into a pan and boil it and add rice as well as salt.
3. Cover for ten minutes.
4. Your dish is ready to be served.

10.9 Tonkatsu

Cooking Time: 15 minutes

Serving: 4

Ingredients:
- Pork loin, one pound
- Eggs, two
- Bread crumbs, half cup
- Cabbage, one

Instructions:

1. Slash the fat rimming one side of the loin cutlet to keep the meat from curling when deep fried.
2. Sprinkle salt and pepper both sides of each cutlet.
3. Dredge each in flour, then dip into beaten eggs and press into bread crumbs to coat both sides.
4. Heat a large skillet with about half inch of oil until hot.
5. Deep-fry until golden brown, about five minutes, turning them once or twice. Drain the cutlets on paper towels and cut the pork into bite-size strips that can be eaten with chopsticks.
6. Arrange the pork on a platter lined with the shredded cabbage, and garnish with lemon wedges.
7. Serve your preferred sauce on the side for dipping, or pour it over the pork and cabbage.

10.10 Wagashi

Cooking Time: 30 minutes

Serving: 3

Ingredients:

- Shiro-an, one cup
- Water, half cup
- Sugar, half cup
- Rice flour, one cup

Instructions:

1. Combine the water, sugar, and rice flour.
2. Stir this in with 600 grams of the shiroan and heat over medium heat.

3. You should end up with a tacky dough that can be shaped with your fingers.
4. Let it cool down.
5. Make into various shapes.
6. Your dish is ready to be served.

10.11 Japanese Matcha Green Tea

Cooking Time: 5 minutes

Serving: 1

Ingredients:

- Matcha tea leaves, one tsp.
- Water, one cup

Instructions:

1. Mix all the ingredients together and then let it boil for five minutes.
2. Drain the tea. Your tea is ready.

Chapter 11: Japanese Vegetarian Recipes

Japan is known for its variety of vegetarian cuisine, Japanese love vegetables, and tend to make more vegetarian meals. Following are some amazing vegetarian recipes:

11.1 Kenchin Vegetable Soup

Cooking Time: 30 minutes

Serving: 3

Ingredients:

- Dashi, one cup
- Mix vegetables, one cup
- Taro, half cup
- Abura age, one cup
- Mirin, two tbsp.
- Soy Sauce, one tbsp.
- Salt, as required
- Sesame oil, two tbsp.

Instructions:

1. Begin by peeling your daikon, burdock and carrot, and then cut them into bite sized chunks.
2. Scrub the taro well with a vegetable brush, making sure any dirt is removed.
3. In a bowl, soak the abura age in hot water to remove any excess oil, and then slice into bite sized pieces.
4. Add the dashi, vegetables and abura age fried tofu to a pan and bring to boil. Add the soy sauce, mirin, salt and sesame oil, and simmer until the vegetables are tender and soft.
5. Serve and garnish with the spring onion.

11.2 Vegan Japanese Omelette

Cooking Time: 10 minutes

Serving: 2

Ingredients:

- Vegan mayo, as required
- Wheat flour, one cup
- Nori, one
- Soy sauce, one tsp.
- Water, one cup
- Salt and pepper to taste
- Oil, two tbsp.

Instructions:

1. In a large mixing bowl, combine all ingredients and stir together so you have a thick dough.

2. Heat a drop of oil in a frying pan and heat on high.
3. Add a scoop of dough and flatten.
4. Reduce flame to medium heat and gently sear each side of the omelette for five minutes.
5. Serve your dish with vegan mayo.

11.3 Japanese Vegetable Pancake

Cooking Time: 25 minutes

Serving: 2

Ingredients:
- Dashi, half cup
- Eggs, two
- Bacon slices, three
- Okonomiyaki sauce, as required
- Mayyonaise, two tbsp.
- Cabbage, half cup
- Green onion, as required
- Flour, one tbsp.

Instructions:
1. Mix the flour, dashi, egg and cabbage in a large bowl.
2. Heat oil in large pan over medium heat, pour in mixture, flatten, top with the bacon slices and cook until golden brown on both sides, about ten minutes per side.
3. Top with okonomiyaki sauce, mayonnaise, and green onion slices.
4. Your dish is ready to be served.

11.4 Vegetarian Japanese Curry

Cooking Time: 30 minutes

Serving: 4

Ingredients:
- Mixed vegetables, two cups
- Green Onions, chopped, three
- Ginger, grated, half tsp.
- Tomato puree, one cup
- Vegetable broth, two cups
- Salt and pepper as required
- Soy Sauce, one tbsp.

Instructions:
1. Mix all the ingredients together, and let it simmer for thirty minutes.
2. Your meal is ready to be served.

11.5 Vegetable Tempura

Cooking Time: 10 minutes

Serving: 2

Ingredients:
- Plain flour, four tbsp.
- Mix vegetables, one cup
- Mayonnaise, half tsp.
- Water, two tbsp.

Instructions:
1. Place the flour, and add icy cold water and mayonnaise.
2. Set aside in fridge until all ingredients and oil are ready.
3. Fill a deep pan or deep-fryer with vegetable oil and heat until 180 degrees.
4. Add each ingredient to the batter individually to coat them and put them into the oil.
5. Fry each ingredient.
6. Your dish is ready to be served with your preferred sauce.

11.6 Japanese Edamame

Cooking Time: 10 minutes

Serving: 2

Ingredients:
- Edamame, one cup
- Soy Sauce, one tbsp.
- Sesame oil, one tsp.
- Salt and pepper to taste

Instructions:
1. Boil edamame for a few minutes.
2. In a pan over high heat, add sesame oil.
3. When the oil is hot, almost smoking, add edamame pods and fry for two minutes.
4. Add soy sauce and stir until the sauce is evaporated.

5. Season with salt and lots of black pepper.
6. Your dish is ready to be served.

11.7 Japanese Eggplant Curry

Cooking Time: 30 minutes

Serving: 4

Ingredients:

- Eggplant, two
- Green Onions, chopped, three
- Ginger, grated, half tsp.
- Tomato puree, one cup
- Vegetable broth, two cups
- Salt and pepper as required
- Soy Sauce, one tbsp.

Instructions:

1. Mix all the ingredients together, and let it simmer for thirty minutes.
2. Your meal is ready to be served.

11.8 Mushroom and Tofu Potstickers

Cooking Time: 15 minutes

Serving: 5

Ingredients:

- Sesame oil, two tbsp.
- Mushrooms, one cup
- Red pepper, half tsp.

- Cabbage, half cup
- Wonton wrappers, ten
- Scallions, half cup
- Ginger and garlic paste, half tsp.
- Olive oil, two tbsp.
- Tofu, one block
- Soy Sauce, one tbsp.

Instructions:

1. Heat a frying pan and add the olive oil.
2. Sauté the crumbled tofu, mushrooms, cabbage, ginger, and garlic for a few minutes.
3. When the tofu and mushrooms are almost cooked, add the scallions, soy sauce, sesame oil, and optional red pepper flakes, stirring well to combine.
4. Add the mixture to wonton wrappers and then steam them for five minutes.
5. Your dish is ready to be served with your preferred sauce.

11.9 Vegetable Teppanyaki

Cooking Time: 10 minutes

Serving: 2

Ingredients:

- Mixed vegetables, two cups
- Sesame oil, two tbsp.
- Salt and pepper to taste
- Cooking wine, two tbsp.

- Soy Sauce, one tbsp.

Instructions:
1. In a skillet over high heat, add two tablespoon oil.
2. Add carrots and cook until almost tender.
3. Add the rest of the vegetables and stir fry.
4. Pour in soy sauce and cooking wine.
5. Season with salt and pepper.
6. Your meal is ready to be served.

11.10 Naturally Sweet Red Bean Daifuku

Cooking Time: 10 minutes

Serving: 6

Ingredients:
- Sweet red beans, two tbsp.
- Caster sugar, two tbsp.
- Rice flour, two cups
- Potato starch, one cup

Instructions:
1. Place the sweet red beans in a small saucepan and pour enough water to cover the red peas.
2. Bring it to simmer over low heat and cook for ten minutes.
3. Place the red beans in a mixing bowl and add sugar and water.
4. Cover your hand with katakuriko potato starch and spread the mochi dough out with your hand.

5. Place the Swedish red peas over the mochi dough and fold the mochi dough in half.
6. Close the mochi ends at the top with your well dusted finger and shape it into a nice round shaped daifuku mochi.
7. Your dish is ready to be served.

11.11 Japanese Carrot Pickles

Cooking Time: 5 hours

Serving: 3-4

Ingredients:
- Rice vinegar, half cup
- Sugar, two tbsp.
- Sesame seeds, as required
- Carrots, two cups

Instructions:
1. In a large cup, whisk together the rice vinegar and sugar until it dissolves completely.
2. Pour the vinegar mixture over all of the carrots, and leave it for five hours.
3. Sprinkle sesame seeds on top and serve.

11.12 Mango Mochi

Cooking Time: 20 minutes

Serving: 5-6

Ingredients:
- Potato starch, two tbsp.

- Water, as required
- Rice flour, one cup
- Green Onions, chopped, three
- Mongo bites, one cup
- Whipped cream, one cup
- Sugar, two cups
- Cream stabilizer one tbsp.

Instructions:
1. In a small cup, add sugar and cream stabilizer.
2. In another bowl, add whipping cream and blend with an electric hand mixer for a few seconds. Then add the sugar mix.
3. Add the whipped cream in the moulds.
4. Place the mango bits on the cream. Then cover with the remaining whipped cream.
5. In a bowl, add glutinous rice flour, sugar and water.
6. Heat over medium heat, stir constantly, until smooth and silky.
7. Spread the potato starch onto your working surface or chopping board.
8. Pull out one filling from the freezer.
9. Pull the edges of the mochi disc over the filling so as to cover it.
10. Your dish is ready to be served.

11.13 Japanese Green Avocado Salad

Cooking Time: 10 minutes

Serving: 2

Ingredients:

- Cucumber, one
- Snowpeas, half cup
- Avocado, one
- Cabbage, half
- Green salad dressing, half cup
- Salt and pepper, per taste

Instructions:

1. Bring a small saucepan of water to a boil and blanch the snowpeas.
2. Peel the cucumber and slice into very thin rounds.
3. For the dressing, whisk all the ingredients together in a small bowl.
4. Combine all the green ingredients in a large bowl, pour the dressing over the top and gently toss with your hands to coat them.
5. Your dish is ready to be served.

11.14 Sweet Potatoes and Avocado Green Salad

Cooking Time: 10 minutes

Serving: 2

Ingredients:

- Sweet potato, one
- Avocado, one
- Green salad dressing, half cup
- Salt and pepper to taste
- Cucumber, one

Instructions:

1. Boil the sweet potato for ten minutes.
2. Cut into pieces and mix the rest of the ingredients.
3. Your dish is ready to be served.

11.15 Japanese Baked Sweet Potato

Cooking Time: 30 minutes

Serving: 3

Ingredients:

- Sweet potatoes, three
- Soy Sauce, one tbsp.
- Sesame oil, two tbsp.
- Salt and pepper, to taste

Instructions:

1. Cut the sweet potatoes into half and add the rest of the ingredients on it.
2. Bake it at 180 degrees for ten minutes.
3. Your dish is ready to be served.

11.16 Japanese Fried Rice

Cooking Time: 30 minutes

Serving Size: 4

Ingredients:

- Fish sauce, two tbsp.
- Egg, one
- Soy sauce, half cup
- Cooked Japanese rice, three cups
- Tomatoes, two
- Cilantro, half cup
- Salt and pepper, to taste
- Vegetable oil, two tbsp.
- Toasted walnuts, half cup
- Chicken breast, eight ounces
- Onion, one
- Scallions, half cup
- Minced garlic, one tsp.

Instructions:

1. Heat a large nonstick pan over high heat.
2. Meanwhile, season chicken lightly with salt and pepper.
3. When the pan is very hot, add two tsp of the oil.
4. When the oil is hot, add the chicken and cook on high until it is browned all over and cooked through.

5. Remove chicken from pan and set aside, add the eggs, pinch of salt and cook a minute or two until done.
6. Add the remaining oil to the pan and add the onion, scallions and garlic.
7. Sauté for a minute, add the chili pepper if using, tomatoes and stir in all the rice.
8. Add the soy sauce and fish sauce stir to mix all the ingredients.
9. Keep stirring a few minutes, and then add egg and chicken back to the wok.
10. Adjust soy sauce if needed and stir well another 30 seconds.
11. Your dish is ready to be served.

11.17 Kenchinjiru

Cooking Time: 30 minutes

Serving: 3

Ingredients:
- Dashi, one cup
- Mix vegetables, one cup
- Taro, half cup
- Abura age, one cup
- Mirin, two tbsp.
- Soy Sauce, one tbsp.
- Salt, as required
- Sesame oil, two tbsp.
- Japanese seven spice, two tbsp.

- Sesame oil, two tbsp.
- Sake, one tsp.
- Tofu, one block.

Instructions:

1. Mix all the ingredients together and let it simmer for thirty minutes straight.
2. Serve and garnish with the spring onion.

The recipes mentioned in this chapter are very easy to make and will fill your craving needs for delicious Japanese cuisine.

Conclusion

Japanese Cuisine is known for its variety of dishes and its vast combination of rare spices that are usually grown only in Japan. This cuisine has been out there from the 18th century but has entered the United States of America from the times when trade began between the two countries, and Japanese people started to move in to America for various purposes.

Today, Japanese cuisine is not only liked by Japanese people residing all over the world but also by other people that live in America. There are various restaurant chains and eateries that make delicious Japanese food but what is better than cooking your favorite meals all by yourself at home.

This book contains all the details that you need to know regarding Japanese cuisine. You can get to know about its history, the different spices that are used in Japanese meals and their various health benefits. So, now you have all the knowledge you need to start cooking Japanese food on your own. This book also contains more than 100 different recipes that include breakfast, lunch, dinner, soups, salads, sweets, traditional as well as vegetarian meals. So, do not wait more, start cooking from today and eat your favorite Japanese healthy and yummy meals at home.

Printed by Amazon Italia Logistica S.r.l.
Torrazza Piemonte (TO), Italy